Crave Radiance

Other Books by Elizabeth Alexander

Poetry

The Venus Hottentot
Body of Life
Antebellum Dream Book
American Sublime
Miss Crandall's School for Young Ladies and Little Misses of Color
　　(with Marilyn Nelson)

Chapbooks

Poems in Conversation and a Conversation (with Lyrae Van Clief-Stefanon)
Praise Song for the Day

Essays

The Black Interior
Power and Possibility: Essays, Interviews, Reviews

Editor

Love's Instruments by Melvin Dixon
The Essential Gwendolyn Brooks

Crave Radiance

New and Selected Poems 1990–2010

Elizabeth Alexander

Graywolf Press

The Venus Hottentot was originally published in 1990 by the University Press of Virginia and reissued in 2004 by Graywolf Press.
Body of Life was originally published in 1996 by Tia Chucha Press.
Antebellum Dream Book was originally published in 2001 by Graywolf Press.
American Sublime was originally published in 2005 by Graywolf Press.
Miss Crandall's School for Young Ladies and Little Misses of Color (co-authored with Marilyn Nelson) was originally published in 2007 by Wordsong.
"Praise Song for the Day" was originally published as a chapbook in 2009 by Graywolf Press.

This publication is made possible by funding provided in part by a grant from the Minnesota State Arts Board, through an appropriation by the Minnesota State Legislature, a grant from the National Endowment for the Arts, and private funders. Significant support has also been provided by Target; the McKnight Foundation; and other generous contributions from foundations, corporations, and individuals. To these organizations and individuals we offer our heartfelt thanks.

NATIONAL ENDOWMENT FOR THE ARTS

MINNESOTA STATE ARTS BOARD

WELLS FARGO

TARGET®

Published by Graywolf Press
250 Third Avenue North, Suite 600
Minneapolis, Minnesota 55401

www.graywolfpress.org

Published in the United States of America

ISBN 978-1-55597-568-5

2 4 6 8 9 7 5 3 1
First Graywolf Printing, 2010

Library of Congress Control Number: 2010922921

Cover design: Julie Metz Design

Cover art: Alma Woodsey Thomas, *Wind and Crepe Myrtle Concerto*, 1973. Used with permission of the Smithsonian American Art Museum, Washington, DC / Art Resource, NY.

For Ficre, Solomon, and Simon,

my three hearts

Contents

From *Antebellum Dream Book* (2001)

From *American Sublime* (2005)

From *Miss Crandall's School for Young Ladies and Little Misses of Color* (2007)

New Poems

The Venus Hottentot

(1990)

The Venus Hottentot

(1825)

CUVIER

Science, science, science!
Everything is beautiful

blown up beneath my glass.
Colors dazzle insect wings.

A drop of water swirls
like marble. Ordinary

crumbs become stalactites
set in perfect angles

of geometry I'd thought
impossible. Few will

ever see what I see
through this microscope.

Cranial measurements
crowd my notebook pages,

and I am moving closer,
close to how these numbers

signify aspects of
national character.

Her genitalia
will float inside a labeled

pickling jar in the Musée
de l'Homme on a shelf

above Broca's brain:
"The Venus Hottentot."

Elegant facts await me.
Small things in this world are mine.

2.

There is unexpected sun today
in London, and the clouds that
most days sift into this cage
where I am working have dispersed.
I am a black cutout against
a captive blue sky, pivoting
nude so the paying audience
can view my naked buttocks.

I am called "Venus Hottentot."
I left Capetown with a promise
of revenue: half the profits
and my passage home: A boon!
Master's brother proposed the trip;
the magistrate granted me leave.
I would return to my family
a duchess, with watered-silk

dresses and money to grow food,
rouge and powders in glass pots,
silver scissors, a lorgnette,
voile and tulle instead of flax,
cerulean blue instead
of indigo. My brother would
devour sugar-studded non-
pareils, pale taffy, damask plums.

That was years ago. London's
circuses are florid and filthy,
swarming with cabbage-smelling
citizens who stare and query,
"Is it muscle? Bone? Or fat?"
My neighbor to the left is
The Sapient Pig, "The Only
Scholar of His Race." He plays

at cards, tells time and fortunes
by scraping his hooves. Behind
me is Prince Kar-mi, who arches
like a rubber tree and stares back
at the crowd from under the crook
of his knee. A professional
animal trainer shouts my cues.
There are singing mice here.

"The Ball of Duchess DuBarry":
In the engraving I lurch
toward the *belles dames,* mad-eyed, and
they swoon. Men in capes and pince-nez
shield them. Tassels dance at my hips.
In this newspaper lithograph
my buttocks are shown swollen
and luminous as a planet.

Monsieur Cuvier investigates
between my legs, poking, prodding,
sure of his hypothesis.
I half expect him to pull silk
scarves from inside me, paper poppies,
then a rabbit! He complains
at my scent and does not think
I comprehend, but I speak

English. I speak Dutch. I speak
a little French as well, and
languages Monsieur Cuvier
will never know have names.
Now I am bitter and now
I am sick. I eat brown bread,
drink rancid broth. I miss good sun,
miss Mother's *sadza.* My stomach

is frequently queasy from mutton
chops, pale potatoes, blood sausage.
I was certain that this would be
better than farm life. I am
the family entrepreneur!
But there are hours in every day
to conjure my imaginary
daughters, in banana skirts

and ostrich-feather fans.
Since my own genitals are public
I have made other parts private.
In my silence I possess
mouth, larynx, brain, in a single
gesture. I rub my hair
with lanolin, and pose in profile
like a painted Nubian

archer, imagining gold leaf
woven through my hair, and diamonds.
Observe the wordless Odalisque.
I have not forgotten my Khoisan
clicks. My flexible tongue
and healthy mouth bewilder
this man with his rotting teeth.
If he were to let me rise up

from this table, I'd spirit
his knives and cut out his black heart,
seal it with science fluid inside
a bell jar, place it on a low
shelf in a white man's museum
so the whole world could see
it was shriveled and hard,
geometric, deformed, unnatural.

West Indian Primer

for Clifford L. Alexander, Sr.
1898–1989

"On the road between Spanish Town
and Kingston," my grandfather said,
"I was born." His father a merchant,
Jewish, from Italy or Spain.

In the great earthquake the ground split
clean, and great-grandfather fell
in the fault with his goat. I don't know
how I got this tale and do not ask.

His black mother taught my grand-
father figures, fixed codfish cakes
and fried plantains, drilled cleanliness,
telling the truth, punctuality.

"There is no man more honest,"
my father says. Years later
I read that Jews passed through my
grandfather's birthplace frequently.

I know more about Toussaint
and Hispaniola than my own
Jamaica and my family tales.
I finger the stories like genie

lamps. I write this West Indian primer.

Ladders

Filene's department store
near nineteen-fifty-three:
An Aunt Jemima floor
display. Red bandanna,

apron holding white rolls
of black fat fast against
the bubbling pancakes, bowls
and bowls of pale batter.

This is what Donna sees
across the "Cookwares" floor,
and hears "Donessa?" *Please,*
this can not be my aunt.

Father's long-gone sister,
nineteen-fifty-three. "Girl?"
Had they lost her, missed her?
This is not the question.

This must not be my aunt.
Jemima? Pays the rent.
Family mirrors haunt
their own reflections.

Ladders. Sisters. Nieces.
As soon a live Jemima
as a buck-eyed rhesus
monkey. Girl? Answer me.

Zodiac

You kissed me once and now I wait for more.
We're standing underneath a swollen tree.
A bridge troll waits to snatch me if I cross.
Your bicycle handles are rusted blue.

My mouth has lost its flavor from this kiss.
I taste of warm apple. My lips are fat.
If these blossoms fall they'll mark our faces:
Gold shards of pollen or flower-shaped dents.

Is it bird wings that bat between my legs?
Is there a myth for trolls? Bulfinch says no.
My mother has a friend who reads the stars.
I am fourteen. "My dear, you look in love."

Your fingers stained dull orange from the bike.
Svetlana eyes and hands, no crystal ball.
White ripe blossoms on a trembling tree.
Again, I think. *I want you to kiss me.*

The Dirt-Eaters

Southern Tradition of Eating Dirt Shows
Signs of Waning
        —headline, *The New York Times*, 2/14/84

tra
dition
wanes
I read
from North
ern South:
D.C.

Never ate
dirt
but I lay
on Great-
grandma's
grave
when I
was small.

"Most cultures
have passed
through
a phase
of earth-
eating
most pre
valent today
among
rural
Southern
black
women."

Geo
phagy:
the practice
of eating
earthy matter
esp. clay
or chalk.

(Shoe-
boxed dirt
shipped North
to kin)

The gos
sips said
that my great-
grand
ma got real
pale when she
was preg
nant:

"Musta ate
chalk,
Musta ate
starch, cuz
why else
did her
babies
look
so white?"

The Ex
pert: "In ano
ther gener
ation I
sus
pect it will dis
appear al
together."

Miss Fannie Glass
of Creuger, Miss.:
"I wish
I had
some dirt
right now."

Her smile
famili
ar as the
smell
of
dirt.

House Party Sonnet: '66

Small, still. Fit through the bannister slit.
Where did our love go? Where did our love go?
Scattered high heels and the carpet rolled back.
Where did our love go? Where did our love go?
My brother and I, tipping down from upstairs
Under the cover of "Where Did Our Love Go?"
Cat-eyed Supremes wearing siren-green gowns.
Pink curls of laughter and hips when they shake
Shake a tambourine *where did our love go?*
Where did our love go? Where did our love go?
Stale chips next morning, shoes under the couch,
Smoke-smelling draperies, water-paled Scotch.
Matches, stray earrings to find and to keep—
Hum of invisible dancers asleep.

Nineteen

That summer in Culpeper, all there was to eat was white:
cauliflower, flounder, white sauce, white ice cream.
I snuck around with an older man who didn't tell me
he was married. I was the baby, drinking rum and Coke
while the men smoked reefer they'd stolen from the campers.
I tiptoed with my lover to poison-ivied fields, camp vans.
I never slept. Each fortnight I returned to the city,
black and dusty, with a garbage bag of dirty clothes.

At nineteen it was my first summer away from home.
His beard smelled musty. His eyes were black. "The ladies love my hair,"
he'd say, and like a fool I'd smile. He knew everything
about marijuana, how dry it had to be to burn,
how to crush it, sniff it, how to pick the seeds out. He said
he learned it all in Vietnam. He brought his son to visit
after one of his days off. I never imagined a mother.
"Can I steal a kiss?" he said, the first thick night in the field.

I asked and asked about Vietnam, how each scar felt,
what combat was like, how the jungle smelled. He listened
to a lot of Marvin Gaye, was all he said, and grabbed
between my legs. I'd creep to my cot before morning.
I'd eat that white food. This was before I understood
that nothing could be ruined in one stroke. A sudden
storm came hard one night; he bolted up inside the van.
"The rain sounded just like that," he said, "on the roofs there."

Omni-Albert Murray

1. OVERTURE

> *"Obviously there is much to be said for the conscious*
> *cultivation and extension of taste, but there is also something*
> *to be said for the functional reaction to artistic design*
> *(and honeysuckles) as normal elements of human existence."*
> —Albert Murray

(three four)   The ancestors are humming: *Write a poem, girl.*
Turn the volume up, they say. Loud-talking. Talking loud.
On piano someone plays a boogie-woogie run:
Omni-Albert Murray   Omni Omni   Albert Murray.

In my mind and in his I think a painting is a poem.
A tambourine's a hip shake and train whistle a guitar.
Trains run North/South home their whistles howling Afro. . . . Am.
Black and blue   Blue   Afro-blue blue-black and blue blew blew

I can picture Bearden with his magazines and scissors.
I can see guitar shapes, curves like watermelon rinds.
Will I find names like Trueblood and the shapes for my collage?
Omni-Albert Murray   Omni Omni   Albert Murray.

2. ELLINGTONIA

> *"So much goes on in a Harlem airshaft. You hear fights,*
> *you smell dinner, you hear people making love. . . . You see*
> *your neighbor's laundry. You hear the janitor's dogs. . . .*
> *One guy is cooking dried fish and rice and another guy's got*
> *a great big turkey. . . . Jitterbugs are jumping up and down*
> *always over you, never below you."*
> —Duke Ellington

I might have jitterbugged at the Renaissance 'room,
thrown upside down by some zoot-suited don
in a vicuña coat, smell of Barbasol—
I might have been a barfly with her wig turned 'round.

I conjure smoke-blue clubs from family tales,
names, like "Do Nothing 'til You Hear from Me."
Duke's square-toed leather shoes, his droop-lid eyes,
his—This is a black and tan fantasy.

Not shoes, not conjure, shaving cream, cologne.
"Tootie for Cootie" unafraid of rhyme.
Bold music, bold as sunflowers. Rhyme is real.
Blow smoke rings when you say "Mood Indigo."

3. INTERLUDE

Albert Murray do they call you Al
or Bert or Murray or "Tuskeegee Boy"?
Who are the Omni-ones who help me feel?
I'm born after so much. Nostalgia hurts.

4. STELLA BY STARLIGHT

*(after the tune, played by Monty Alexander on
piano and Othello Molyneaux on steel drum)*

Red hair in summertime,
ashy toes, dust-knuckled,
the slim curve of autumn
in sight. In summertime
rhiney, shedding burnt skin,
petticoats, pantaloons.
I'm a rusty-butt sun-
baby, summer is gone.

No more corn and no blue-
berries. Sweet tomatoes
overripe. No more ice
blocks with *tamarindo,*
sweaty love in damp white
sheets, sunflowers, poppies,
salt in summertime,
sun-stoked bones. Summer jones.

Starlight cool as the edge
of fall. "Stella by Star-
light" steals stars for letters.
Each *l* and each *t* pricks
the sky like a star or
a steel drum quiver on
a note 'til it shimmer.
Who is Stella? Summer's

5. BEARDEN AT WORK

*"Regardless of how good you might be at whatever else you did,
you also had to get with the music."*
—Romare Bearden

Paper-cutting rhythm, snips of blue foil
falling onto water-colored paper,
colored people into place. Eye divines
arrangement, hands slide shifting paper shapes.
Panes of color learned from stained-glass windows,
pauses   spacing   rests   from Fatha Hines.

Odysseus is blue. He can't get home.
In Bearden's planes: collage on board, shellac.
Watch Dorothy, children, enter Oz.
Look, Daddy, color! No more white and black.
This is the year of the color TV.
Odysseus is blue and now is black.

New York City at Christmastime. Christmas
tree-shapes like Bearden in Bearden blue.
Tin stars falling on a yellow paper
trumpet. Blue sucked in, blues blown back out.
Black folks on ice skates shine like Christmas trees.
New York glitters like a new idea.

6. CODA

Omni: having unrestricted, universal range.
Coda: a concluding passage, well-proportioned clause.
On piano someone plays a boogie-woogie run:
Omni-Albert Murray   Omni   Omni   Albert Murray.

Robeson at Rutgers

Hard to picture, but these Goliath trees
are taller still than Robeson. Outside
vast plate windows in this lecture hall,
I imagine him running down autumn fields,
see his black thighs pumping that machinery
across chalk-painted lines.

                      He loved the woman
in the lab, Eslanda, who saw order
in swimming circles on inch-wide slides, who
made photographs. I picture her standing
in darkness, led by red light, bathing paper
in broth, extracting images. Did this woman smile
to watch white paper darken, to pull wet
from the chemicals Paul Robeson's totem face?

Van Der Zee

(1886–1983)

I say your name: James Van Der Zee
for dancing girls and barbershops
when names were names. That was a time.

From Dutch your name is "by the sea."
A boy in endless Lenox snow
you're open-eyed, lean as the trees.

Waiter and elevator jobs.
Your cigar fingers, rolled-up sleeves,
the sent-away-for photo kit:

Those brownstone textures, marcelled hair,
iron faces, gathered drapery,
smooth foreheads, porcelain basins,

hoary beards, brocaded chairs.
Brown knees and calves in smooth nylons,
straw flower baskets, blacksmith's flames.

Father Divine or Daddy Grace
the blind will see   the lame will walk
Garvey's white plumes and epaulets.

Big Jack Johnson. Bojangles.
Sunshine Sammy. Harlem "Y. M."
Somebody's boy scout son salutes,

a brownskin time-steps. Funerals,
babies. The New York Black Yankees.
"Hey! It's the picture-takin' man!"

Signed "JAMES VANDERZEE N.Y.C."
Black stories in brown photographs—
You're drinking ginger ale and Scotch.

Bearden

One eye is larger than her two black hands.
Sunday hats. Brass trumpets. Flowered dresses.
A woman's holler. River or guitar.

Gigantic ham-hands. Open, singing mouths.
Brown purple mouths, huge hands, and wet-bean eyes.
These opaque eyes are looking straight at you.
Women's haunches. The black backs of skulls.

Black spaces sucking in a breath, like jazz.
Low moons. Women taking tin-tub baths.

Deadwood Dick

Come on and slant your eyes again,
O Buffalo Bill.
   —Carl Sandburg

Colored cowboy named Nat Love,
They called him Deadwood Dick.
A black thatch of snakes for hair,
Close-mouthed. Bullet-hipped.

One knee bent like his rifle butt,
Just so. Rope. Saddle. Fringe.
Knock this white boy off my shoulder.
Stone-jawed, cheekboned man.

Mama, there are black cowboys.
A fistful of black crotch.
Deadwood Dick: Don't fuck with me.
Black cowboy. Leather hat.

Painting

(Frida Kahlo)

I've cropped the black hair Diego loves.
The swatches swarm about my feet.

I've cut a window in my forehead.
See? Diego, skull and bones,

magenta, nighttime fever-dreams.
His walls and walls of scenes of work,

brown women bare, female lilies.
I am spider-eyed among monkeys!

A year in bed   I still see blood
in crimson   olive   orchid   jade.

Look at my heart beat! See my veins!
As I lie bleeding in the street

a woman's sack of gold dust splits:
my bloody body gleaming gold—

I wish I could have painted it!
I will witness my own cremation
because ash is as lovely as fire.

Monet at Giverny

Iris and haystack. Japanese footbridge.
Knobby poplars, vertical and blue
Or yellow. Floating blossoms of pink light.
Water lilies bloom and bloom and bloom.

There are no frogs. There is no princess here.
Planes of edgeless violet, scraps of light.
Blurred green flames and fingernails of light.
He painted this same pond year after year.

The sky becomes the water, then the deep.
Xanthopsia: Monet saw the light yellow.
Physicians, operations, spectacles—
"Disgusting, I see everything in blue."

Farewell to You

Each man on this slow train
has Bearden's Brueghel face,
his clean crown, putty-smooth,
eyes wise, no trace

of the colors, shapes behind them,
of paper cut to palms
or rump curves or half-moons,
or rooster-comb.

Through Newark, apple blossoms
line train tracks to the church,
and broken eyes of windows
as these cars lurch

past oil drums, blue and yellow,
like the blues singer's dress,
past empty boxcars stacked
like tenement windows,

or like piano keys
awaiting Fatha Hines,
Willie the Lion Smith.
Sound unwinds,

stanzas float in this notebook
at angles to the page
like the angles of music
in a Bearden clef.

Nausicaa makes jelly:
a green anemone,
snake-hips unmoored
in a blue-black sea.

These stanzas on the page
discarded strips from your collage
salvaged like America:
creole montage.

Honor the artist's vision
of a vast world, black and blue.
Beloved Romare Bearden:
Farewell to you.

Penmanship

I notice older women have better penmanship
than I do. Smooth and even, free from stray hairs,
readable, learned by copying lessons onto
wide-ruled paper in marbleized notebooks, the product
of discipline, of knowing what was expected
and then doing it. I would have done it too, then.

My blue cursive crazes the white letter paper.
"I cannot read you!" friends shriek back, in neater
hand as intimate as pica or block print.
In grade school I painted wild-eyed art class sunsets
with tempera colors absent from nature, finger paints.
One bold boyfriend returned typed letters to sender.

Long before teacher-training school, Grandmother's friends
made miles and miles of *m*'s with camel-humps that
grazed the middle, dotted line, humps swelled with plenty
of water to go across deserts and deserts
of vast first halves of alphabets, each uppercase *q*
a perfect, backward 2. Commas swam off the page.

A favorite teacher's purple curlicues startle
my essays with snarled lines and no Rosetta stone.
I'm trying to neaten up my hand, my open-
classroom, flower-power hand. Am I creeping in
from the margins? Am I now current, legible,
when gold-foil stars are not enough, nor penmanship?

Letter: Blues

Those Great Lake Winds
blow all around:
I'm a light-coat man
in a heavy-coat town.
　　　　—Waring Cuney

Yellow freesia arc like twining arms;
I'm buying shower curtains, smoke alarms,
And Washington, and you, Love—states away.
The clouds are flat. The sky is going grey.

I'm fiddling with the juice jug, honey pot,
White chrysanthemums that I just bought.
At home, there is a violet, 3-D moon
And pachysandra vines for me to prune,

And old men with checkered shirts, suspenders,
Paper bags and Cutty bottles, menders
Of frayed things and balding summer lawns,
Watching TV baseball, shelling prawns.

The women that we love! Their slit-eyed ways
Of telling us to mind, pop-eyed dismays.
We need these folks, each one of them. We do.
The insides of my wrists still ache with you.

Does the South watch over wandering ones
Under different moons and different suns?
I have my mother's copper ramekin,
A cigar box to keep your letters in.

At least the swirl ceilings are very high,
And the Super's rummy, sort of sly.
I saw a slate-branched tree sway from the roots—
I've got to buy some proper, winter boots.

So many boxes! Crates and crates of books.
I must get oil soap, bleach, and picture hooks.
A sidewalk crack in Washington, D.C.
Will feed my city dirt roots. Wait for me.

Boston Year

My first week in Cambridge a car full of white boys
tried to run me off the road, and spit through the window,
open to ask directions. I was always asking directions
and always driving: to an Armenian market
in Watertown to buy figs and string cheese, apricots,
dark spices and olives from barrels, tubes of paste
with unreadable Arabic labels. I ate
stuffed grape leaves and watched my lips swell in the mirror.
The floors of my apartment would never come clean.
Whenever I saw other colored people
in bookshops, or museums, or cafeterias, I'd gasp,
smile shyly, but they'd disappear before I spoke.
What would I have said to them? Come with me? Take
me home? Are you my mother? No. I sat alone
in countless Chinese restaurants eating almond
cookies, sipping tea with spoons and spoons of sugar.
Popcorn and coffee was dinner. When I fainted
from migraine in the grocery store, a Portuguese
man above me mouthed: "No breakfast." He gave me
orange juice and chocolate bars. The color red
sprang into relief singing Wagner's *Walküre*.
Entire tribes gyrated and drummed in my head.
I learned the samba from a Brazilian man
so tiny, so festooned with glitter I was certain
that he slept inside a filigreed, Fabergé egg.
No one at the door: no salesmen, Mormons, meter
readers, exterminations, no Harriet Tubman,
no one. Red notes sounding in a gray trolley town.

A Poem for Nelson Mandela

Here where I live it is Sunday.
From my room I hear black
children playing between houses
and the El at a Sabbath rattle.
I smell barbecue from every direction
and hear black hands tolling church bells,
hear wind hissing through elm trees
through dry grasses

              On a rooftop of a prison
in South Africa Nelson Mandela
tends garden and has a birthday,
as my Jamaican grandfather in Harlem, New York
raises tomatoes and turns ninety-one.
I have taken touch for granted: my grandfather's hands,
his shoulders, his pajamas which smell of vitamin pills.
I have taken a lover's touch for granted,
recall my lover's touch from this morning
as Mandela's wife pulls memories through years
and years

            My life is black and filled with fortune.
Nelson Mandela is with me because I believe
in symbols; symbols bear power; symbols demand
power; and that is how a nation
follows a man who leads from prison
and cannot speak to them. Nelson Mandela
is with me because I am a black girl
who honors her elders, who loves
her grandfather, who is a black daughter
as Mandela's daughters are black
daughters. This is Philadelphia
and I see this Sunday clean.

Today's News

Heavyweight champion of the world Mike Tyson
broke his fist in a street brawl in Harlem
at three A.M. outside an all-night clothing store
where he was buying an 800-dollar, white
leather coat. The other dude, on TV, said,
"It was a sucker punch." Muhammad Ali said
Tyson ain't pretty enough to be heavyweight
champion of the world. Years ago a new Ali
threw his Olympic gold into the Ohio
River, said he'd get it when black people were truly
free in this country. In South Africa there is a dance
that says   we are fed up   we have no work   you have
struck a rock. I saw it on today's news.

I didn't want to write a poem that said "blackness
is," because we know better than anyone
that we are not one or ten or ten thousand things
Not one poem   We could count ourselves forever
and never agree on the number. When the first
black Olympic gymnast was black and on TV I called
home to say it was colored on channel three
in nineteen-eighty-eight. Most mornings these days
Ralph Edwards comes into the bedroom and says, "Elizabeth,
this is your life. Get up and look for color,
look for color everywhere."

From

Body of Life

(1996)

Stravinsky in L.A.

In white pleated trousers, peering through green
sunshades, looking for the way the sun is red
noise, how locusts hiss to replicate the sun.
What is the visual equivalent
of syncopation? Rows of seared palms wrinkle
in the heat waves through green glass. Sprinklers
tick, tick, tick. The Watts Towers aim to split
the sky into chroma, spires tiled with rubble
nothing less than aspiration. I've left
minarets for sun and syncopation,
sixty-seven shades of green which I have
counted, beginning: palm leaves, front and back,
luncheon pickle, bottle glass, etcetera.
One day I will comprehend the different
grades of red. On that day I will comprehend
these people, rhythms, jazz, Simon Rodia,
Watts, Los Angeles, aspiration.

The Josephine Baker Museum

1. East St. Louis (1918)

Mama danced
a glass
of water balanced
on her head.

"Someone raped
a white woman!"
We ran
at night,
next day
heard tell

of eyes
plucked out,
of scalps
pulled clean,
a bloody sky.

That day
God showed
his face,
grey and shaggy,
in the rain clouds.

2. Costumes

The black and white checked overalls
I wore off the boat at Le Havre. Wired skirts
whose trains weigh fifty pounds. Furling,
curling headpieces and hourglass-
shaped gowns.

Schiaparellis and Poirets! The green suede
Pilgrim shoes and orange jacket,
Harlem-made. The lime chiffon!
The one with egrets
painted on.

I'm sick of *touts le bananes.* Ici,
my uniform: French Air Force, fray-spots
blackened back with ink. And here,
the diamond necklace,
for my glorious Chiquita.

3. *The Wig Room*

A gleaming black sputnik of hair.
A solid figure-eight of hair, glazed black.
Crows' wings of hair, a waist-length switch.

Black profiteroles of mounded hair.
Hair like an Eiffel Tower, painted black.
A ziggurat of patent leather hair.

Black crowns to be taken on and off, that live
in the room when the lights go out, a roomful
of whispering Josephines, a roomful
of wigs in the dark.

4. Ablutions

In the cinema Mammy hands Scarlett
white underthings to cover her white skin.
I am both of them and neither, tall,
tan, terrific, soaking in my tub of milk.

What would it mean to be me on stage
in a bathtub soaping, singing my French
chansons with one pointed foot with painted toes
suggesting what is underneath, suggesting

dusky, houri dreams and is she really
naked? Do they really want to see
the nappy pussy underneath that sweats
and stinks and grinds beneath bananas,

turns to seaweed in the tub? What if
I let my hair go back, or dressed
more often as a man? What if I let myself
get fat? What would it mean to step out

of the bathtub onto the stage and touch
myself, do to myself what I do to myself
in the bedroom when only my animals
watch? What would I be to my audience then?

(Sigh) Come here, baby. Dry me off.

5. *Diva Studies*

What is original, what
is facsimile? The boys
in the dressing room are showing
me how to skin my hair down flat
like patent leather, black as that.
I show them how to paint eyeballs
on their eyelids to look bright
from the last row, how I line
my eyes like the Egyptian cat.
We carry on, in that dingy,
musky, dusty room overhung
with fraying costumes, peeling
sequins, shedding feathers, mules
with broken heels, mending glue, eye-
lash glue, charcoal sticks and matches,
brushes and unguents and bottles of oil.
The dressing room is my schoolhouse.
My teachers and men more woman
than actual women, and I
am the skinny sixteen-year-old
whose hair is slicked flat because
Congoleum burned it off.
I cross my eyes and knock my knees,
am somehow still a diva.
The boys swoop past and are rare.
The beauty is how this strange
trade works. The truth of it is,
we are fabulous.

Yolande Speaks

Yolande Du Bois was the only
daughter of W.E.B. Du Bois

I know some call him
"Doctor Dubious."

I hear how people
talk. I know who's

called my marriage
counterfeit. I know

who thinks me stupid.
I would love

the peace and quiet
of stupidity,

having witnessed
the hot hiss of

true intelligence,
a white noise, a

camphor that over-
takes the globe.

I have laughed
at my father's gloves

and spats. My pace
is my own. I am

a sputtering
cadmium light

turning on
like the R.K.O.

Radio Tower.

Fugue

Virginia Woolf, incested
through her childhood, wrote
that she imagined herself
growing up inside a grape.
Grapes are sealed and safe.
You wouldn't quite float
in one; you'd sit locked
in enough moisture to keep
from drying out, the world
outside through gelid green.
Picture everyone's edges
smudged. Picture everyone
a green as delicate
as a Ming celadon. Pic-
ture yourself a mollusk
with an unsegmented body
in a skin so tight and taut
that you'd be safe. You could
ruminate all night about
the difference between "taut"
and "tight," "molest" and "incest."
"Taut" means tightly-drawn,
high-strung. What is tight
is structured so as not to
permit passage of liquid
or gas, air, or light.

The Texas Prophet

I am the Texas Prophet who is now in Baltimore.
God blesses those that see me and I'm coming to your town.
I guarantee you without fail a straight and one-way blessing.
I come to bring you luck and by your popular demand.

I'm bringing Mojo hands for those of you can't win for losing.
All manner of disease is healed. Cash money falls like rain.
If I were you I would come early. He can't stay all night.
Those who know me know I am no money-hungry Prophet.

I am the Texas Prophet who is now in Baltimore.
I'm bringing good luck talismans and guarantee my work.
Keep looking up   keep looking up   His help is on the way.
Yours in spirit and in love The Prophet John C. Bates.

Talk Radio, D.C.

Leave fatback and a copper penny
on a wound 'til it draw out the poison,
'til the penny turn green.

Tobacco's what works on a bee-sting,
but for poison ivy—I'm serious, now—
catch your first morning urine in your hands
and splash it on that rash.

When they had the diptheria epidemic
I was burning up with fever, burning and burning.
When the doctor left the house, my grandmother
snuck in the back door with a croaker sack of mackerel.
She wrapped me all up in that salt mackerel.
The next morning, my fever had broke
and the fish was all cooked.

Passage

Henry Porter wore good clothes for his journey,
the best his wife could make from the leftover
cambric, shoes stolen from the master. They
bit his feet, but if he took them off he feared
he'd never get them on again. He needed
to look like a free man when he got there.
Still in a box in the jostling heat,
nostrils to a board pried into a vent,
(a peephole, too, he'd hoped, but there was only
black to see) there was nothing to do
but sleep and dream and weep. Sometimes the dreams
were frantic, frantic loneliness an acid
at his heart. Freedom was near but un-
imaginable. Anxiety roiled inside
of him, a brew which corroded his stomach,
whose fumes clamped his lungs and his throat.
When the salt-pork and cornbread were finished
he dreamed of cream and eggs but the dreams
made him sick. He soiled himself and each time
was ashamed. He invented games, tried to
remember everything his mother
ever told him, every word he hadn't
understood, every vegetable he'd ever
eaten (which was easy: kale, okra, corn,
carrots, beans, chard, yams, dandelion greens),
remember everyone's name who had ever
been taken away. The journey went that way.
When he got there, his suit was chalky
with his salt, and soiled, the shoes waxy with blood.
The air smelled of a surfeit of mackerel.
Too tired to weep, too tired to look through
the peephole and see what freedom looked like,
he waited for the man to whom he'd shipped
himself: Mister William Still, Undertaker,

Philadelphia. He repeated the last
words he'd spoken to anyone: good-bye
wife Clothilde, daughter Eliza,
best friend Luke. Good-bye, everyone, good-bye.
When I can, I'll come for you. I swear,
I'll come for you.

Summertime

Where we live there are caged peacocks
in summertime, heavy in the heat,
bald-headed, dragging their tails, which,
once a season, they unfurl. Objects
wrinkle in the heat waves rising
from the pavement. A dead rat
in the back alley gets a proper
burial from a girl who can flip
her eyelids inside out, and at
the funeral I wear my white
go-go boots and sing "I Gotta Be Me."
We buy coverless comic books
cut-rate, impossibly red
vending machine pistachios
which stain our hands. A hydrant
illicitly opened, kids riding
the hard spray, caught in the rainbow
of water. On television,
Senators talk, talk, talk.
A Wham-O Superball bounces
off a sidewalk crack and into
the cosmos. A red rubber planet
could bounce to the sky and stick.

Washington Étude

After rain, mushrooms
appear in the park
but you can not eat them.

1967,
the year of the locust.
They come to Northwest

Washington by millions
and for days I crunch
shed husks beneath my feet

as they rattle and hiss
their rage from the trees.
Baby teeth bite baby

onion grass and honey-
suckle nipples, tiny
tongue balancing

the clear, sweet drops.
I am a humming-
bird, a cat who laps

cream from a bowl.
Dandelions
are yellow one day,

white the next. A mud-
puddle surrounded
by brambles and black-

berries is where God lives.
Buttercups under
my chin tell me all

I need to know. Nothing
blue occurs naturally
in Washington, someone

says, and I believe it.
I'm put to bed
when it's still light

and hear other children
playing out my window,
watch daylight bow,

regard the flare
of blooming stars,
the cicada's maraca.

Apollo

We pull off
to a road shack
in Massachusetts
To watch men walk

on the moon. We did
the same thing
for three two one
blast off, and now

we watch the same men
bounce in and out
of craters. I want
a Coke and a hamburger.

Because the men
are walking on the moon
which is now irrefutably
not green, not cheese,

not a shiny dime floating
in a cold blue,
the way I'd thought,
the road shack people don't

notice we are a black
family not from there,
the way it mostly goes.
This talking through

static, bouncing in space-
boots, tethered
to cords is much
stranger, stranger

even than we are.

What I'm Telling You

If I say, my father was Betty Shabazz's lawyer, the poem can
go no further. I've given you the punchline. If you know
who she is, all you can think about is how and what you
want to know about me, about my father, about Malcolm,
especially in 1990 when he's all over t-shirts and medallions,
but what I'm telling you is that Mrs. Shabazz was a nice
lady to me, I loved her name for the wrong reasons,
SHABAZZ! and what I remember is going to visit her
daughters in 1970 in a dark house with little furniture and
leaving with a candy necklace the daughters gave me, to
keep. Now that children see his name and call him Malcolm
Ten, and someone called her Mrs. Ex-es, and they don't
really remember who he was or what he said or how he
smiled the way it happened when it did, and neither do I,
I think about how history is made more than what happened
and about a nice woman in a dark house filled with
daughters and candy, something dim and unspoken,
expectation.

Butter

My mother loves butter more than I do,
more than anyone. She pulls chunks off
the stick and eats it plain, explaining
cream spun around into butter! Growing up
we ate turkey cutlets sauteed in lemon
and butter, butter and cheese on green noodles,
butter melting in small pools in the hearts
of Yorkshire puddings, butter better
than gravy staining white rice yellow,
butter glazing corn in slipping squares,
butter the lava in white volcanoes
of hominy grits, butter softening
in a white bowl to be creamed with white
sugar, butter disappearing into
whipped sweet potatoes, with pineapple,
butter melted and curdy to pour
over pancakes, butter licked off the plate
with warm Alaga syrup. When I picture
the good old days I am grinning greasy
with my brother, having watched the tiger
chase his tail and turn to butter. We are
Mumbo and Jumbo's children despite
historical revision, despite
our parents' efforts, glowing from the inside
out, one hundred megawatts of butter.

Compass

I.

I swing
the thin tin
arm to mark
an arc
from pole
to pole: my
mother's compass
spans the world.
It marks
the globe from east
to west on this
white paper as
I twirl
the compass,
hear the hush
of graphite:
a horizon.

II.

It feels freest
at its widest set,
held just by a pin-
prick on the page,
moored and precarious,
like Matthew Henson's flag.

III.

Even the dogs died.
His Eskimo grandchildren cried

when, years later, the black man
they prayed was a Henson

came looking to figure
what makes a man hazard

ten lifetimes of snow. Hayden
imagined your arguments, hunger,

delirium. The fur of your hood
frames your brown face like petals or rays.

To stand where the top of the world curves.
To look all around in that silence.

To breathe in cold air that has never
Been squandered, breathe out again.

To breathe in cold air, to breathe
in . . . out . . .

breathe in

Frank Willis

I am in the four percent
of adults 18-29 who told
George Gallup they know
"a lot" about Watergate.
"Watergate" was the building
near the Howard Johnson's where
we'd go when school let out for summer
and eat clam strips. Water-
gate was where we stopped
in carpool one year to fetch
the sickly boy for day camp,
where I danced in toe shoes
to the Beach Boys, in shame.
Growing up in Washington
I rode D.C. Transit, knew Senators,
believed the Washington Monument
was God's pencil because my friend
Jennifer said so, never went
to the Jefferson Memorial,
climbed the stone rhino
at the Smithsonian, cursed tourists,
took exquisite phone messages
for my father, a race man,
who worked for the government—
I held his scrawled hate mail to the light.

I don't care now that Chuck Colson
has a prison ministry, or that G.
Gordon Liddy ate a rat.
The summer I was eleven Water-
gate was something I watched
with my grandmother on TV like the best
soap opera but also like something
she would have called "civic," the things

you had to know. Today in some way
I somehow care that Frank Willis lives
with his mother, without employ,
was arrested for stealing
a $12 pair of sneakers, told *Jet*
it was "a total mix-up," somehow know
there is meaning in *Jet*'s tending the fate
of this man who saw the tape
on the office door latch. Cog, cog,
cog in the wheel of history, Frank
Willis in *Jet* these years later,
like the shouted spray-paint on an empty
garage in my parents' back alley:
"Aaron Canaday," his name alone
enough, and then a sentence,
a song: "Slick was Here-O."

Family Stone

We drive "The Nutmeg State" in summer.
Daddy sings "Your Feets Too Big." You lie!
we scream, there's no such song. You lie! we scream, at
"Buttermilk Sky." We beg for more,
then beg for WAVZ-13. The O'Jays sing
"Backstabbers," then Sly Stone.

                      We believe
it's a family affair, believe in someone
named Sly, something called a family stone because
it's on the radio today—

   and so on
   and so on
   and scooby dooby dooby

—but this other language, Daddy singing
"your pedal extremities are collosal,"
and who ever tasted buttermilk, and why
is he called "Hoagy," is something else

all together. These old-heads who are
my parents come from New York City,
from another tribe. We are the DeeCee kids
and think we don't speak jazz. But we will dream
that night, after wide eyes to stars sharp
as the word "Connecticut," dream of mammoth
feet with painted toes, buckets of clabber, sirens.

Six Yellow Stanzas

1.

Didn't know what to do
at the Boulé Ball,
so I put on a Mardi Gras mask
of a smile and watched
those Creoles second-line,
light yellow faces, bright
white kerchiefs waving
back and forth
made languid light.

2.

Langour.
I lay back
in the bucket seat,
for the first time
let a yellow boy
kiss me and kiss me and kiss me,
talk that talk.

3.

I don't know how
to talk that talk.
I am visiting friends
of a family friend.
These Creole ways
are something I
have never seen
before or since.
Yellow boys squire me
to glittering clubs
where I am the coal
in the Christmas stocking.
Curious, curious
yellow me. I can't
tell who among
these creamy
freesia women—
they all are.
They let some men
be dark, like the one
they call Dark Gable,
who could talk
that talk the best.
The club is dark.
Some men are dark.
The women shine
and glitter. Me.

4.

Photograph:
my yellow moon-
pie face, yellow baby
screaming in the middle of the bed.
You could pass for Spanish,
a man says, as a compliment.
You a high-yella gal, and I like that,
says a suitor. Yellow!

I dreamed I had a yellow baby.
In the dream I didn't feed it.
It dried flat on the blacktop
like an old squashed frog.
I tried to revive it with lemonade
by the dropperful,
but that was the end
of my yellow dream baby.

5.

My thigh next to your thigh.
Your black thigh
(your dark brown thigh)
next to my black thigh
(which is "yellow"
and brown, and black).
Sunless flesh or sunshine flesh.
I startle myself
with my yellowness
next to your black
but say none of this,
and lick your skin 'til yellow-
black sparks fly,
a hive of bumblebees
which hum at your body
and do not sting.

6.

Egg yolk, crocus, buttercup, butter,
dandelion, sunflower, sunbeam, sun,
chicken fat, legal pads, bumble-bee stripes,
a bowl full of lemons, grapefruit peel,
iris hearts, pollen, the Coleman's mustard can,
the carpet and sheets in my childhood bedroom:
things that are yellow and yellow alone.

Blues

I am lazy, the laziest
girl in the world. I sleep during
the day when I want to, 'til
my face is creased and swollen,
'til my lips are dry and hot. I
eat as I please: cookies and milk
after lunch, butter and sour cream
on my baked potato, foods that
slothful people eat, that turn
yellow and opaque beneath the skin.
Sometimes come dinnertime Sunday
I am still in my nightgown, the one
with the lace trim listing because
I have not mended it. Many days
I do not exercise, only
consider it, then rub my curdy
belly and lie down. Even
my poems are lazy. I use
syllabics instead of iambs,
prefer slant- to the gong of full rhyme,
write briefly while others go
for pages. And yesterday,
for example, I did not work at all!
I got in my car and I drove
to factory outlet stores, purchased
stockings and panties and socks
with my father's money.

To think, in childhood I missed only
one day of school per year. I went
to ballet class four days a week
at four-forty-five and on
Saturdays, beginning always
with plie, ending with curtsy.

To think, I knew only industry,
the industry of my race
and of immigrants, the radio
tuned always to the station
that said, Line up your summer
job months in advance. Work hard
and do not shame your family,
who worked hard to give you what you have.
There is no sin but sloth. Burn
to a wick and keep moving.

I avoided sleep for years,
up at night replaying
evening news stories about
nearby jailbreaks, fat people
who ate fried chicken and woke up
dead. In sleep I am looking
for poems in the shape of open
Vs of birds flying in formation,
or open arms saying, I forgive you, all.

Affirmative Action Blues

(1993)

Right now two black people sit in a jury room
in Southern California trying to persuade
nine white people that what they saw when four white
police officers brought batons back like
they were smashing a beautiful piñata was
"a violation of Rodney King's civil rights,"
just as I am trying to convince my boss not ever
to use the word "niggardly" in my presence again.
He's a bit embarrassed, then asks, but don't you know
the word's etymology? as if that makes it
somehow not the word, as if a word can't batter.
Never again for as long as you live, I tell him,
and righteously. Then I dream of a meeting
with my colleagues where I scream so loud the inside
of my skull bleeds, and my face erupts in scabs.
In the dream I use an office which is overrun
with mice, rats, and round-headed baby otters
who peer at me from exposed water pipes (and somehow
I know these otters are Negroes), and my boss says,
Be grateful, your office is bigger than anyone
else's, and maybe if you kept it clean you wouldn't
have those rats. And meanwhile, black people are dying,
beautiful black men my age, from AIDS. It was amazing
when I learned the root of "venereal disease"
was "Venus," that there was such a thing as a disease
of love. And meanwhile, poor Rodney King can't think straight;
what was knocked into his head was some addled notion
of love his own people make fun of, "Can we all
get along? Please?" You can't hit a lick with a crooked
stick; a straight stick made Rodney King believe he was
not a piñata, that amor vincit omnia.
I know I have been changed by love.
I know that love is not a political agenda, it lacks sustained

72

analysis, and we can't dance our way out of our constrictions.

I know that the word "niggardly" is "of obscure etymology"
   but probably derived from the French Norman, and that
   Chaucer and Milton and Shakespeare used it. It means
   "stingy," and the root is not the same as "nigger," which
   derives from "negar," meaning black, but they are
   perhaps, perhaps, etymologically related. The two gs
   are two teeth gnawing; "rodent" is from the Latin "rodere"
   which means "to gnaw," as I have said elsewhere.

I know so many things, including the people who love me and the people
   who do not.

In Tourette's syndrome you say the very thing that you are thinking, and
   then a word is real.

These are words I have heard in the last 24 hours which fascinate me:
   "vermin," "screed," "carmine," and "niggardly."

I am not a piñata, Rodney King insists. Now can't we all get along?

Haircut

I get off the IRT in front of the Schomburg Center for Research in Black Culture after riding an early Amtrak from Philly to get a haircut at what used to be the Harlem "Y" barbershop. It gets me in at ten to ten. Waiting, I eat fish cakes at the Pam Pam and listen to the ladies call out orders: bacon-biscuit twice, scrambled scrambled fried, over easy, grits, country sausage on the side. Hugh is late. He shampoos me, says "I can't remember, Girlfriend, are you tender-headed?" From the chair I notice the mural behind me in the mirror. I know those overlapped sepia shadows, a Renaissance rainforest, Aaron Douglas! Hugh tells me he didn't use primer and the chlorine eats the colors every day. He clips and combs and I tell him how my favorite Douglas is called *Building More Stately Mansions,* and he tells me how fly I'd look in a Salt 'n' Pepa 'do, how he trained in Japan.

Clip clip, clip clip. I imagine a whoosh each time my hair lands on the floor and the noises of small brown mammals. I remember, my father! He used to get his hair cut here, learned to swim in the caustic water, played pool and basketball. He cuts his own hair now. My grandfather worked seventy-five years in Harlem building more stately mansions. I was born two blocks away and then we moved.

None of that seems to relate to today. This is not my turf, despite the other grandfather and great-aunt who sewed hearts back into black chests after Saturday night stabbings on this exact corner, the great-uncle who made a mosaic down the street, both grandmothers. What am I always listening for in Harlem? A voice that says, "This is your place, too," as faintly as the shadows in the mural? The accents are unfamiliar; all my New York kin are dead. I never knew Fats Waller but what do I do with knowing he used to play with a ham and a bottle of gin atop his piano; never went to Olivia's House of Beauty, but I know Olivia, who lives in St. Thomas, now, and who exactly am I, anyway, finding myself in these ghostly, Douglas shadows while real ghosts walk around me, talk about my stuff in the subway, yell at me not to butt the line, beg me, beg me for my money?

What is black culture? I read the writing on the wall on the side of the "Y" as I always have: "Harlem Plays the Best Ball in the World." I look in the mirror and see my face in the mural with a new haircut. I am a New York girl; I am a New York woman; I am a flygirl with a new haircut in New York City in a mural that is dying every day.

Judge Gets Grandma to Whip Offender

Instead of sending a drug offender to prison, a judge took off his belt and had the 18-year-old defendant's grandmother whip the young man.

The defendant, Jamel Washington, needed "discipline, in the home and in the schools," the judge, Frank Eppes, said on Friday.

"I said, 'Grandmama, don't you think he needs a whipping?'" the judge said. "She said he needed one."

The whipping was conducted by the grandmother, 63-year-old Victoria Washington Ellis.

For Miriam

Fields of iridescent, butter-lettuce green:
Germany a bright tail behind me
as I ride the train into Amsterdam's

impossible diphthongs, yellow or blue
*g*s stopping words in new places. Poets
travel and make poems about travel,

grasp at their travels as I do here.
"Land" was a word for "elsewhere" I used
in childhood, for storybook places where

other people lived. Italy: gondoliers
in tight, striped shirts, land of red and green noodles.
England: land of kings and queens, Elizabeth's

ermine-trimmed cape, her scepter and tiara,
Henry tearing at an outsized drumstick.
Germany: Adolph Hitler, mustachioed

Lucifer from another land, the Black
Forest where the Nazis had their revels,
my grandmotther said. Now I have seen

Berlin's bullet-pocked buildings, the proud, scarred
church downtown, bolts of starry yellow fabric
stamped "JUDE" in black, train schedules and ledgers

a rage of numbers, a cemetery
of Saras. In a bombed-out lot at dusk, art
made of rubble rose from smoke and rap music.

I've drunk green, herb-tinted beer; eaten bags
of local cherries and light-brown bread;
been jostled in a market jazzed with

turmeric, pistachios, raw fish,
hemp and honey soaps, silver trinkets;
sweated in a hammam where Turkish women

dance naked for each other in the steam.
I know, this is hardly the sum of it.
In my Berlin dreams, Jesse Owens' legs

are a brown flurry speeding past the Führer
in the name of another tribe, my own.
Here we talked about history, history,

history, which country forgets more, denies
more, and what is to be salvaged, in whose name?
Star-white jasmine, train-tracks without end—

This is what I have seen in your country, friend.

L.A. by Night

We're in a postcard, driving
down Hollywood Boulevard:
the car has fins, the palm trees
are pink, we wear cat-eye sun-
glasses in the L.A. night
glare, the neon chatter, blurred
white lights of speeding cars.
We are speed and light, flames
and fingers; all night
is a fistful of minutes,
a fast car, stars.

                Later,
we will make love loudly
in a room which belongs
to neither one of us, a room
strewn with our clothes and our
belongings. We will repeat
what we love most, our tongues
wise and specific. You'll say
I am a glow-worm, a cobalt star.

In L.A., the palm trees
are more ancient than they look
and objects closer than they
seem, but no city's myths
can explain our two moon faces
in the dark. We are zooming
and loud, fast hands, a bright
light, a magnificent
planet, L.A. by night.

Harlem Birthday Party

When my grandfather turned ninety we had a party
in a restaurant in Harlem called Copeland's.
Harlem restaurants are always dim to dark and this
was no exception. Daddy would have gone downtown
but Baba, as we called him, wanted to stay
in the neighborhood, and this place was "swanky."
We picked him up in his house on Hamilton Terrace.
His wife, "poor Minnette," had Alzheimer's disease
and thought Hordgie, who was not dead, was dead. She kept
cluck-clucking, "Poor Hordgie," and filling with tears.
They had organized a block watch on Hamilton
Terrace, which I was glad of; I worried always
about old people getting mugged; I was afraid
of getting old myself and knocked down in the street;
I was afraid it would happen to my grandfather.

My father moves fast always but in Harlem
something clicks into his walk which I love watching.
We fussed about taking a car, about parking;
in the end some walked, some drove, and the restaurant
parked the car for us. They treated my grandfather
like a Pope or like Duke Ellington. We ate salad,
fried chicken, mashed potatoes, broccoli, chocolate
cake, and Gustavo, who was then my boyfriend, cut Minnette's
meat for her and that became one of the things I would cite
forever when people asked me, how did you know
you wanted to marry him? I remember looking
at all the people at the party I had never seen,
and thinking, my grandfather has a whole life
we know nothing about, like at his funeral,
two years later, when a dreadlocked man about my age
went on and on about coming to Harlem
from Jamaica, they all said, talk to Mister Alex-
ander, and they talked, and my grandfather scolded,

advised, and today the young brother owns a patty stand
in Brooklyn. Who ever knew this young man, or all the rest?

The star appearance at Copeland's, besides my father,
was my grandfather's wife's cousin, Jane Tillman Irving,
who broadcast on WCBS all-news radio.
What is a Harlem birthday party without a star?
What is a black family without someone
who's related to someone else who is a little
bit famous, if only to other black people?

And then good-bye, and then good-bye, and back
to New Haven, Washington, and Philadelphia,
where I lived with Gustavo. We walked downtown
after the party to Macy's to get feather pillows
on sale, and then we took Amtrak home. I cannot think
about this party without thinking how glad I am
we had it, that he lived long and healthy, that two years
later he was gone. He was born in Jamaica,
West Indies, and he died in Harlem, New York.

Body of Life

1. 1990

One by one 'til
I'm the only one
left in the photo
we took in Gay Paree,
trill the final syl-
lable, thrill to
pretending we're
the Revue Negre,
funking so fiercely
our black clothes stained
our curvature, fab-
ulous flames let loose
in the city of lights.

One by one you leave
the picture, nix nix nix,
my moonpie face left
shining there. Au Revoir,
or like they say
in Sula, "Vwah!", bright
as a bottle, the beau-
tiful children are
leaving me to trill
the final syllable,
this beautiful-
ugly world.

2. 1983

The other girls taught shy me to be a diva,
to preen, to plump my titties up like they did,
to work it. We danced. We wanted the body
of life and I lived for a year in that
body, the body of life, in D.C.,
in the African diaspora:
Chocolate City.

          That was my slut year.
All the men I didn't sleep with, all I did,
all the lunch dates, all the dinners, all
the whistles on the streets of Chocolate
City, all the men who called me Baby,
called me Girl, like the one who made me tuna-
fish and tried to suck my breasts, then asked
me to type up his resume. My buzzer
in the middle of the night, my phone, a man
who greased me head to toe with Lubriderm,
a Cape Verdean who appeared on buses
and trains as if by divination, sketched
me naked, never spent the night. I told
one man how much I loved Betty Carter
and he said, I hope you're not one of those
bulldaggers. A lonely Nigerian
who cooked fufu and groped me on the sofa,
his across-the-ocean wife and daughter
watching from their picture frames.
Rum and dancing, too many things in my mouth,
genitals cobbled with passion or disease, bright
clitoris a phantom limb, remembering—

I moved away to Boston and would call
you for the update: Renee was a samba
star at Brasil Tropical, shimmied
on Brazilian TV. Denise graduated

school and made the foreign service, moved
to Jamaica, to a bungalow, with
a man and a maid named Pansy. "Who's sick?"
I'd ask and you'd tell me, and who died,
and one day you said, "And I'm living with AIDS."

There was Kemron in Kenya.
You were saving to get it.
You met with a support group
of other black men. You had
a Dominican boyfriend,
same as me. Mostly you felt
OK, but you hated
your medicine. You were fat,
but you still took class.
No, Tyrone wasn't sick. But David was dead.

It was Njambi who called me to say,
you were back in shape. You performed
for the visiting Eminence of Senegal,
the next day went into the hospital,
the next day died. It made a romantic
story, but you're still gone. "I love when you call me
because you're alive, " you said once,
one of your few friends still alive.
I'm writing this poem to say how we were,
that we danced and fucked and sweated, loved
ourselves and each other, lived fiercely,
knew joy. I'm writing to say,
I got lucky, you were my friend, you
knew me as a girl, I am a woman,
now, with my little piece of your story,
the year of the body of life.

3. 1994

(In my neighborhood now I watch women who are lovely
at a distance and lurid up close cross the street serving much
runway, much attitude, and I am Ovaltine, a walrus, no
longer sharp and spangled. In my half-sleep I hear teeth
sucking from the dead, the divas awakening to coach me:
Never let on you are less than fabulous, one says, hissing
in disgust at all the home-training I've forgotten, so I pull
myself together and whistle, a bald, brown, and beautiful
Yul Brynner signing Deborah Kerr's lines: *Whenever I feel
afraid, I hold my head erect, and whistle a happy tune, so
no one will suspect I'm afraid.*

Life is only momentarily fearless; life is only for a moment
full of cures; the body, as always, tells the round, bald truth
when my stomach grips to say, no cure in sight.)

Blues

Wrigley illuminates
the night sky violet,

indigo city tonight,
Chicago, city

surrounded by Magikist lips,
baci baci baci

benedicting the expressways.
"Sixty-watt gloom" suffused

Hayden's Detroit, the South
Side's similar neon face.

I elegize cities
and leave them, cities

my imagined Atlantises.
Tonight, all Chicago

is singing the blues.
Autumn came today,

winter next, always.
Elegy, indigo, blues.

Equinox

Now is the time of year when bees are wild
and eccentric. They fly fast and in cramped
loop-de-loops, dive-bomb clusters of conversants
in the bright, late-September out-of-doors.
I have found their dried husks in my clothes.

They are dervishes because they are dying,
one last sting, a warm place to squeeze
a drop of venom or of honey.
After the stroke we through would be her last
my grandmother came back, reared back and slapped

a nurse across the face. Then she stood up,
walked outside, and lay down in the snow.
Two years later there is no other way
to say, we are waiting. She is silent, light
as an empty hive, and she is breathing.

At the Beach

Looking at the photograph is somehow not
unbearable: My friends, two dead, one low
on T-cells, his white T-shirt an X-ray
screen for the virus, which I imagine
as a single, swimming paisley, a sardine
with serrated fins and a neon spine.

I'm on a train, thinking about my friends
and watching two women talk in sign language.
I feel the energy and heft their talk
generates, the weight of their words in the air
the same heft as your presence in this picture,
boys, the volume of late summer air at the beach.

Did you tea-dance that day? Write poems
in the sunlight? Vamp with strangers? There is
sun under your skin like the gold Sula
found beneath Ajax's black. I calibrate
the weight of your beautiful bones, the weight
of your elbow, Melvin,

                    on Darrell's brown shoulder.

Cleaning Out Your Apartment

A fifty-year-old resume
that says you raised delphiniums.
Health through Vegetable Juice,
your book of common prayer,

your bureau, bed, your easy chair,
dry Chivas bottles, mop and broom,
pajamas on the drying rack,
your shoe trees, shoe-shine box.

I keep your wicker sewing kit,
your balsa cufflink box. There's
only my framed photograph to say,
you were my grandfather.

Outside, flowers everywhere,
the bus stop, santeriá shop.
Red and blue, violent lavender.
Impatiens, impermanent, swarm.

Tending

In the pull-out bed with my brother
        in my grandfather's Riverton apartment
my knees and ankles throbbed from growing,
        pulsing so hard they kept me awake—
or was it the Metro North train cars
        flying past the apartment, rocking the walls,
or was it the sound of apartment front doors
        as heavy as prison doors clanging shut?
Was the Black Nation whispering to me
        from the *Jet* magazines stacked on the floor, or
was it my brother's unfamiliar ions
        vibrating, humming in his easeful sleep?
Tomorrow, as always, Grandfather will rise
        to the Spanish-Town cock's crow deep in his head
and perform his usual ablutions,
        and prepare the apartment for the day,
and peel fruit for us, and prepare a hot meal
        that can take us anywhere, and onward.
Did sleep elude me because I could feel
        the heft of unuttered love in his tending
our small bodies, love a silent, mammoth thing
        that overwhelmed me, that kept me awake
as my growing bones did, growing larger
        than anything else I would know?

Leaving

Presence and absence are too absolute
to describe the way you were those last years,
Nana, always there in varying degrees.
One day you sat up and asked about "Doctor
Du Bois's great book" and you were not confused.
In one of your long quiet stretches I dreamed
you were on the cover of *Parade* magazine
in a yellow tunic and yellow leggings
(yes, I know, you never wore yellow)
sitting cross-legged in a field, telling
your secrets of aging well.

                    When you died
we gathered and wept over your body
and stroked your beautiful hair. You're not buried
anywhere, so there's no metaphor to visit.
You told me when I was too young to hear
that you wanted to donate your body
to science, Howard University
Medical School, and then cremation.
The urn is too literal, and anyway,
I don't know where Mom put it. You visit me
still in my dreams, full-blown for moments
then elsewhere   good-bye   and that's
the way it is, now, that's the way it is.

After

It wasn't as deep as I expected,
your grave, next to the grandmother who died
when I was three. I threw a flower in
and fizzled off the scene like carbonation.
My body of course remained but all else
was a cluster of tiny white bubbles
floating up, up, up, to an unseen top.

I wore your vicuna coat and an ill-
fitting cloche from Alexanders. I walked
among the rows, away from the men
covering the coffin, which was when I saw
"X," Malcolm, a few yards down, "Paul Robeson,"
then "Judy Garland" then – the car was waiting
and we had to go.

           The cocktail parties
must be something there! You'd discuss self-help
and the relative merits of Garvey-
ism with Malcolm. Robeson would read
in a corner. Judy, divine in black
clam-diggers, would throw back her head
and guffaw, smoke as many cigarettes
as she wanted.

           Before you died I dreamed
of cocktail parties in your Harlem
apartment where you'd bring all our dead kin
back to life, for me! I was old enough
to drink with you, to wear a cocktail dress.
Like the best movies, the dream was black
and white, except for my grandmother's
lipstick, which was red.

From

Antebellum Dream Book

(2001)

Fugue

1. *Walking (1963)*

after the painting by Charles Alston

You tell me, knees are important, you kiss
your elders' knees in utmost reverence.

The knees in the painting are what send the people forward.

Once progress felt real and inevitable,
as sure as the taste of licorice or lemons.
The painting was made after marching
in Birmingham, walking

into a light both brilliant and unseen.

2. 1964

In a beige silk sari
my mother danced the frug
to the Peter Duchin Band.

Earlier that day
at Maison Le Pelch
the French ladies twisted

her magnificent hair
into a fat chignon
while mademoiselle watched,

drank sugared, milky tea,
and counted bobby pins
disappearing in the thick-

ness as the ladies worked
in silence, adornment
so grave, the solemn toilette,

and later, the bath,
and later, red lipstick,
and later, L'Air de Temps.

My mother without glasses.
My mother in beige silk.
My mother with a chignon.
My mother in her youth.

3. 1968

The city burns. We have to stay at home,
TV always interrupted with fire or helicopters.
Men who have tweedled my cheeks once or twice
join the serial dead.

Yesterday I went downtown with Mom.
What a pretty little girl, said the tourists, who were white.
My shoes were patent leather, all shiny, and black.
My father is away saving the world for Negroes,
I wanted to say

Mostly I go to school or watch television
with my mother and brother, my father often gone.
He makes the world a better place for Negroes.
The year is nineteen-sixty-eight.

4. 1971

"Hey Blood," my father said then
to other brothers in the street.
"Hey, Youngblood, how you doin'?

"Peace and power," he says,
and "Keep on keepin' on,"
just like Gladys Knight and the Pips.

My stomach jumps: a thrill.
Sometimes poems remember small things, like
"Hey, Blood." My father
still says that sometimes.

5. *The Sun King (1974)*

James Hampton, the Sun King
of Washington, D.C.
erects a tinfoil throne.
"Where there is no vision, the people perish."
Altar, pulpit, lightbulbs.

My 14th and "U," my 34 bus, my weekday winos,
my white-robed black Israelites
on their redstone stoops,
my graffiti: "Anna the Leo as 'Ice,'"
my neon James Brown poster
coming to the D.C. Coliseum
where all I will see is the circus,
my one visit to R.K.O. Keith's Theater
to see *Car Wash*
and a bird flew in, and mania,
frantic black shadow on the screen,
I was out of the house in a theater full of black folks,
black people, black movie, black bird,
I was out, I was free, I was at R.K.O. Keith's Theater
at 14th and "U"
and it was not *Car Wash* it was the first
Richard Pryor concert movie
and a bird flew in the screen
and memory is romance
and race is romance,
and the Sun King lives
in Washington, D.C.

Elegy

Motherless, fatherless,
born of no one and everything,

Sun Ra touched down in Birmingham,
The Magic City, city of smokestacks

and tin. He would glitter.
Began departure from Philly,

which is Saturn, in a way.
Said he was no age, never was born.

He's not from no Mars, his sister Mary said.
I peeped through the keyhole. I saw that boy born.

The spaceship left from Birmingham,
city the color of lead, city of trains,

of metal, city of black, black coal.

Overture: Watermelon City

Philadelphia is burning and water-
melon is all that can cool it,
so there they are, spiked
atop a row of metal poles,
rolling on and off pickup trucks,
the fruit that grows longest,
the fruit with a curly tail, the cool fruit,
larger than a large baby, wide
as the widest green behind, wide
vermilion smile at the sizzling metropole.
Did I see this yesterday? Did I dream
this last night? The city is burning,
is burning for real.

When I first moved here I lived two streets over
from Osage, where it happened, twelve streets down.
I asked my neighbors, who described
the smell of smoke and flesh,
the city on fire for real.
How far could you see the flames?
How long could you smell the smoke?
Osage is narrow, narrow
like a movie set: urban eastern seaboard,
the tidy of people who work hard for very little.

Life lived on the porch,
the amphitheater street.
I live here, 4937 Hazel Avenue, West Philly.
Hello, Adam and Ukee,
the boys on that block
who guarded my car, and me.
They called him Ukee because
as a baby he looked
like a eucalyptus leaf.

Hello, holy rollers
who plug in their amps,
blow out the power in the building,
preach to the street from the stoop.
Hello, crack-head next-door neighbor
who raps on my door after midnight
needing money for baby formula,
she says, and the woman
who runs in the street
with her titties out, wailing.
Hello, street. Hello, ladies
who sweep their front porches each morning.
In downtown Philadelphia
there are many lovely restaurants,
reasonably priced.
Chocolate, lemon ice,
and hand-filled cannolis
in South Philly.
Around the corner
at the New Africa Lounge
in West Philadelphia
we sweat buckets
to hi-life and zouk,
we burn.

Early Cinema

According to Mister Hedges, the custodian
who called upon their parents
after young Otwiner and young Julia
were spotted at the matinee
of Rudolph Valentino in *The Sheik*
at the segregated Knickerbocker Theater
in the uncommon Washington December
of 1922, "Your young ladies
were misrepresenting themselves today,"
meaning, of course, that they were passing.
After coffee and no cake were finished
and Mister Hedges had buttoned his coat
against the strange evening chill,
choice words were had with Otwiner and Julia,
shame upon the family, shame upon the race.

How they'd longed to see Rudolph Valentino,
who was swarthy like a Negro, like the finest Negro man.
In *The Sheik,* they'd heard, he was turbaned,
whisked damsels away in a desert cloud.
They'd heard this from Lucille and Ella
who'd put on their fine frocks and French,
claiming to be "of foreign extraction"
to sneak into the Knickerbocker Theater
past the usher who knew their parents
but did not know them.
They'd heard this from Mignon and Doris
who'd painted carmine bindis on their foreheads,
braided their black hair tight down the back,
and huffed, "We'll have to take this up with the Embassy"
to the squinting ticket taker.
Otwiner and Julia were tired of Oscar Michaux,
tired of church, tired of responsibility,
rectitude, posture, grooming, modulation,

tired of homilies each way they turned,
tired of colored right and wrong.
They wanted to be whisked away.

The morning after Mister Hedges' visit
the paperboy cried "Extra!" and Papas
shrugged camel's hair topcoats over pressed pajamas,
and Mamas read aloud at the breakfast table,
"No Colored Killed When Roof Caves In"
at the Knickerbocker Theater
at the evening show
from a surfeit of snow on the roof.
One hundred others dead.

It appeared that God had spoken.
There was no school that day,
no movies for months after.

Visitor

Belo Horizonte

The city rocks at close of day,
buses lumber, workers hustle home.
Sunlight's a silt on these buildings
outside my hotel window. I am high up,
a visitor to this new city, excited
and weary as Lorca or Senghor. Here,
they say it straight: white women
to marry, black women for work,
mulattas for fucking. There are hundreds
of words describing color, skin, and who
I would be in this city is unclear.

A car horn plays "La Cucaracha,"
just like Uptown, USA. Streetlights
and headlights appear like chicken pox.
I could look out this window for hours
at the finishing day, the lancets
and whippets of shiny rose light.
My eyes are a gemologist's, divining
mica from mud, mining iridescence,
a country composed in legible lumens, color.

Days later on the night-flight,
almost West and home, the wide sky wakes.
America becomes visible beneath plush clouds
outside bituminous Pittsburgh,
gray and mottled, gridless, dappled.

Then the clouds clot and we are in heaven.

I am black again. The sky is pale and pink.

My suitcase is full of poems in Portuguese,
beads to protect me that will break in a month,
vacuum-packed coffee beans, ebony fists,
black soap that lathers up creamy, and white.

Geraniums

In my front yard, Negro
flower,

"When Sue Wears Red," Negro
genius behind a picket fence,

nodding heads, blooms
smell spice, not sweet,

burred green splinters,
common weed, edible green—

geraniums in my front yard,
survivors, nigger red.

Islands Number Four

1.

Agnes Martin, *Islands Number Four,*
Repeated ovals on a grid, what appears
To be perfect is handmade, disturbed.
Tobacco brown saturates canvas to burlap,
Clean form from a distance, up close, her hand.
All wrack and bramble to oval and grid.
Hollows in the body, containers for grief.
What looks to be perfect is not perfect.

Odd oval portholes that flood with light.

2.

Description of a Slave Ship, 1789:
Same imperfect ovals, calligraphic hand.
At a distance, pattern. Up close, bodies
Doubled and doubled, serried and stacked
In the manner of galleries in a church,
In full ships on their sides or on each other.
Isle of woe, two-by-two, spoon-fashion,
Not unfrequently found dead in the morning.
Slave ships, the not pure, imperfect ovals,
Portholes through which they would never see home,
The flesh rubbed off their shoulders, elbows, hips.
Barracoon, sarcophagus, indestructible grief
Nesting in the hollows of the abdomen.
The slave ship empty, its cargo landed
And sold for twelve ounces of gold apiece

Or gone overboard. Islands. Aftermath.

Nat Turner Dreams of Insurrection

... too much sense to be raised, and if I was,
I would never be of any service to any one as a slave.
The Confessions of Nat Turner, 1831

Drops of blood on the corn, as dew from heaven.
Forms of men in different attitudes, portrayed in blood.
Numbers, glyphs, on woodland leaves, also in blood.

Freedom: a dipperful of cold well water.
Freedom: the wide white sky.
Dreams that make me sweat.

Beacause I am called, I must appear so, prepare.
I am not a conjurer. Certain marks on my head and breast.
Shelter me, Great Dismal Swamp. A green-blue sky which roils.

Race

Sometimes I think about Great-Uncle Paul who left Tuskegee,
Alabama to become a forester in Oregon and in so doing
became fundamentally white for the rest of his life, except
when he traveled without his white wife to visit his siblings—
now in New York, now in Harlem, USA—just as pale-skinned,
as straight-haired, as blue-eyed as Paul, and black. Paul never told anyone
he was white, he just didn't say that he was black, and who could imagine,
an Oregon forester in 1930 as anything other than white?
The siblings in Harlem each morning ensured
no one confused them for anything other than what they were, black.
They were black! Brown-skinned spouses reduced confusion.
Many others have told, and not told, this tale.
When Paul came East alone he was as they were, their brother.

The poet invents heroic moments where the pale black ancestor stands up
on behalf of the race. The poet imagines Great-Uncle Paul
in cool, sagey groves counting rings in redwood trunks,
imagines pencil markings in a ledger book, classifications,
imagines a sidelong look from an ivory spouse who is learning
her husband's caesuras. She can see silent spaces
but not what they signify, graphite markings in a forester's code.

Many others have told, and not told, this tale.
The one time Great-Uncle Paul brought his wife to New York
he asked his siblings not to bring their spouses,
and that is where the story ends: ivory siblings who would not
see their brother without their telltale spouses.
What a strange thing is "race," and family, stranger still.
Here a poem tells a story, a story about race.

Baby

The doctor handed me a parfait dish
of melting pink and coffee ice cream
and said, "Congratulations! A girl!"
This bewildered me; I had not been
pregnant, but I kissed the dish and put her
in the deep freeze to see if she'd take shape.
I knew there was a baby in there somewhere,
her tiny arms and legs in vaguest outline.
The doctor frowned, then smiled again:
"Congratulations! A boy!" This one
had a mammoth head and a full set
of teeth. I named the babies Vincent and Louise.
Meanwhile, my father fluttered about
the room and discouraged visitors.
My mother-in-law said, "I made you turkey
breast and rice. You didn't eat." My husband
slept deeply on my brother's bunk bed.
I talked about the dream and later thought
about something someone told me, that
giving birth is all about yourself.
I am formless and fanged, boy and girl both,
food and baby at the very same time.

Crash

I am the last woman off of the plane
that has crashed in a cornfield near Philly,

picking through hot metal
for my rucksack and diaper bag.

No black box, no fuselage,
just sistergirl pilot wiping soot from her eyes,

happy to be alive. Her dreadlocks
will hold the smoke for weeks.

All the white passengers bailed out
before impact, so certain a sister

couldn't navigate the crash. O gender.
O race. O ye of little faith.

Here we are in the cornfield, bruised and dirty but alive.
I invite sistergirl pilot home for dinner

at my parents', for my mother's roast chicken
with gravy and rice, to celebrate.

The Toni Morrison Dreams

1.

Toni Morrison despises
conference coffee, so I offer
to fetch her a Starbucks
macchiato grande, with turbinado sugar.

She's delighted, can start her day properly,
draws on her Gauloises,
shakes her gorgeous, pewter dreads,
sips the java that I brought her
and reads her own words:

    Nuns go by as quiet as lust

Everything in silver-gray and black.

2. Workshop

She asks us to adapt
Synge's *Playboy of the Western World*
for the contemporary stage.
She asks us to translate "The Birds."

She asks us to think about clocks,
see the numbers as glyphs,
consider the time we spend watching them

in class, on line, at the hairdresser's.

In class she calls me "Ouidah" and I answer.

"I am the yellow mother
of two yellow boys," she says.
I sit up straight.

Now the work begins, and
Oh
the work is hard.

3.

She does not love
my work, but she loves

my baby, tells me
to have many more.

4. A Reading at Temple University

"Love," she wrote,
and "love" and "love" and "love,"

and "amanuesis," "velvet," "pantry," "lean,"

Shadrack, Solomon, Hagar, Jadine, Plum,

circles   sth   runagate

and then,
she whispered it,

love

"The female seer will burn upon this pyre"

Sylvia Plath is setting my hair
on rollers made from orange-juice cans.
The hairdo is shaped like a pyre.

My locks are improbably long.
A pyramid of lemons somehow
balances on the rickety table

where we sit, in the rented kitchen
which smells of singed naps and bergamot.
Sylvia Plath is surprisingly adept

at rolling my unruly hair.
She knows to pull it tight.
                              Few words.
Her flat, American belly,

her breasts in a twin sweater set,
stack of typed poems on her desk,
envelopes stamped to go by the door,

a freshly baked poppyseed cake,
kitchen safety matches, black-eyed Susans
in a cobalt jelly jar. She speaks a word,

"immolate," then a single sentence
of prophecy. The hairdo done,
the nursery tidy, the floor swept clean

of burnt hair and bumblebee husks.

War

In the dream there was goo,
yellow goo which hurled itself
at unclothed bodies, and burned.
Shower water slowing to a trickle,
mayhem on TV and on the radio.

Dan Rather in slow motion:
We thought they'd attack
a medium-sized city of poor people,
like Philadelphia,
not a mighty city like Chicago.

Tanks, firing with no sound.
Mayhem, a word I've been drawn to
for the last week for no apparent reason,
my newest, pulsing word
in a dream where I do not picture enemies.

Peccant

Maryland State Correctional Facility for Women,
Baltimore County Branch, has undergone a face-lift.
Cells are white and ungraffitied, roomlike, surprisingly airy.
This is where I must spend the next year, eating slop from tin trays,
facing women much tougher than I am, finding out if I am brave.
Though I do no know what I took, I know I took something.

On Exercise Day, walk the streets of the city you grew up in,
in my case, D.C., from pillar to post, Adams-Morgan to Anacostia,
Shaw to Southwest, Logan to Chevy Chase Circles,
recalling every misbegotten everything, lamenting, repenting.

How my parents keen and weep, scheme to spring me,
intercept me at corners with bus tokens, pass keys, files baked in cakes.
Komunyakaa the poet says, don't write what you know,
write what you are willing to discover, so I will
spend this year, these long days, meditating on what I am accused of
in the white rooms, city streets, communal showers, mess hall,
where all around me sin and not sin is scraped off tin trays
into oversized sinks, all that excess, scraped off and rinsed away.

Opiate

A date with Michael Jordan proves
he is a true gentleman, arrives smiling,
bearing a bouquet of red carnations,
driving a modest sports car, in a sober
but stylish navy-blue suit. He grins that grin.
Hello Michael Jordan then off you go,
have your date, then have lovely safe sex,
after which you remember, you are married,
you don't know Michael Jordan, even though
he is your age-mate, and lumbers
off the championship court nowadays
looking much like you do after nursing
your newborn at four in the morning
blue night after inky blue night.

          "Michael Jordan
is the opiate of the masses," comes a voice
at the end of the dream, perhaps John Cameron Swayze
or James Earl Jones as Darth Vader. "Michael Jordan
is the opiate of the masses." Opiates are verboten
for nursing moms like me. Improbable, ominous;
our date was so *Father Knows Best,* so
Mayberry RFD, such a wide, wide grin.
I wake to a foghorn, "Opiate of the masses,"

no memory of the feel of his dark and lovely skin.

After the Gig: Mick Jagger

The baby cries. Mick Jagger swaggers backstage,
lit with sweat. The crowd still screams outside.
He's been second-lining with a gaggle of New Orleans Negroes,
a white parasol, wears toreador pants and is bare-chested, bones.

I've forgiven the Rolling Stones for fetishizing me
and my sisters in "Brown Sugar" and "Some Girls."
Black girls, black girls, black girls.
Why does so much flotsam populate my brain?
Why not ancient Ge'ez, the Mingus discography,

suminagashi paper technique,

something utilitarian?

This is a four weeks postpartum dream. Mick Jagger's
black baby cries again. Thank God, it isn't mine.
Gotta go, love, gotta go, he says,
and shrugs his bony shoulders,
grins that reptile-mammal grin,

picks the baby up, coo-coos,

and then rocks that baby down.

Postpartum Dream #8

In a hail of bazooka fire they drop
her toddler from the second-floor porch.
She knows he'll land in bushes and survive.
They'll leave him for dead. When the shots subside
she'll grab him, shush him, shrink him pocket-sized,
kung-fu fight to the basement crawl space
to plan how to rescue the six-week-old baby.
The toddler thinks she's the mother in all his books,
Mama Tiger, Mama Bear, Mama Elephant: "Mama."
What else is she to do with all that pride?

Look right, look left. She runs head-down, toddler
in her pocket, straight to Foster Care, where
she sweeps away paperwork, storms marble corridors,
high heels clicking past uniformed matrons
and rows of bassinets 'til she sees
the silver arc of her sweet baby's pee.
Baby! My baby! His mouth at the ready,
her nipples stand out from here to St. Louis,
unsexy and mighty, full of that much milk.

Postpartum Dream #12: Appointment

I answered all
the Chief Justice's questions
impeccably, and it wasn't
very hard.

I waited
with my father
for the phone call.

"I guess I'll be
the first black woman
on the Supreme Court
if I get this."

"Damn straight,"
said my dad.

The President
appeared on television
playing golf and smiling.
He has a secret.
His secretary phones
and asks the question.

Maybe I could do it
when the baby
goes to kindergarten. Maybe
I could do it
on alternate Mondays.
Maybe my baby
could gurgle and coo
in a pen in my chambers,
pulling at the curls
on my barrister's wig,
spitting up on my black robes.

Meanwhile,

I'm excited. I turned out
to be a good lawyer, the best,

just like my dad.

The Party

Obi had a big ole party
for his birthday, in New York City,
with an African band called Difunkt.

Harry Belafonte came,
sang "Rum and Coconut Water."
We ate while we rocked to the beat.

You had to dress in costume,
so I came as Nefertiti,
with sandals laced up my ankles

and a papier-mâché crown.
Floating in a pan of water
was a hydroponic baobab tree,

free-floating, without any roots.
The baby inside of me danced,
and thumped so hard my Nefertiti

dress blew up all around me!
And we floated eggs in the water.
At the end of a baobab's life

their trunks explode into water!
Explode, explode, explode,
and the baby inside of me danced.

Orange

The doctor has diagnosed cancer, sees
"shadows" and "masses" in the sad, damp bags
which are my lungs. I have three weeks at best.

I am running through Idlewild airport, wheezing,
as I race to catch the evening flight to Paris.
I want to be bumped up to first class, I have cancer,
want champagne, toasted nuts and extra legroom,
crave comfort, however it comes.

                                Miss one train,
catch another, said a friend's wise mother,
meaning, keep on keeping on, meaning
get back on the horse, meaning it ain't over
'til it's over, 'til the fat lady sings.
Can the baby now quickening inside me
survive on its own? I'd asked the doctor.
This was my first thought, my first such thought.
Yes, he'd reassured me, she'll be tiny,
but babies, like cancers, grow and grow.

I can't run fast enough. I miss that plane.
A man dressed all in orange whisks me
to his mother's, shows his first-edition books,
autobiographies, of Angela Davis, Joe Louis,
Muhammad Ali. Then he lifts his mother's mattress,
displays a million dollars in small bills.
He tells me wise things, wise things I can't remember
but take in like mentholated steam:

                                    I'm dead,
he said, I died at 37. It's not so bad.
I come back when I need to, walk amongst you
leaving signs that I passed through. The dead
wear orange when they come back to visit.
That is how you know which ones we are.

Visitation

Pablo Neruda still lives in my dream,
will discuss with me a better language
for poems both "political" and "personal,"
dandles my poppy-faced baby on his knee,
offers to blurb my latest collection,
prefers English to Spanish this bright afternoon
(but oh how my Spanish glitters in this dream!).
I remember to him his great poems, muses:
Matilde Urrutia, "Amores: Josie Bliss," "Walking Around,"
lines that made the words inside me shift and organize.
He understands why I fall asleep sometimes
when Important Visitors lecture at the University.
Of course you fall asleep, he says, and waves.
Adiós, cariña. You're off to write a poem.

Feminist Poem Number One

Yes I have dreams where I am rescued by men:
my father, brother, husband, no one else.
Last night I dreamed my brother and husband
morphed into each other and rescued me
from a rat-infested apartment. "Run!"
he said, feral scampering at our heels.
And then we went to lunch at the Four Seasons.

What does it mean to be a princess?
"I am what is known as an American Negro,"
my grandmother would say, when "international friends"
would ask her what she was. She'd roller-skate
to Embassy Row and sit on the steps of the embassies
to be certain the rest of the world was there.

What does it mean to be a princess?
My husband drives me at six A.M.
to the airport an hour away, drives home,
drives back when I have forgotten my passport.
What does it mean to be a prince? I cook
savory, fragrant meals for my husband
and serve him, if he likes, in front of the TV.
He cooks for me, too. I have a husband.

In the dream we run into Aunt Lucy,
who is waiting for a plane from "Abyssinia"
to bring her lover home. I am the one
married to an Abyssinian, who is already here. I am the one
with the grandmother who wanted to know the world.
I am what is known as an American Negro princess,
married to an African prince,
living in a rat-free apartment in New Haven,
all of it, all of it, under one roof.

Gift

I dreamed I forgot to say thank you
to someone who gave me a gift.

Amphibious cheekbones and brow, tobacco skin,
white carnation bath, white light in the water.
Then I was clean, and lit out for the territory,

Chicago on a bicycle, splendid metropolis, ghetto heaven,
Humboldt Park, chiquitas, white summer dresses,
vendor alcapurrias, front porch, chicken in the kitchen,
lunch break, back to the Lake,
heal a sad soul in her exhausted body.

He took the pan from me and finished cooking, said, Rest.
Like a man he would disappear—
(An ugly part which does not bear retelling.
Cut the brown part from the fruit and eat the rest.)
—And so I rested.

Insight often disappears but leaves residue,
what you understand and did not know before.
It is not quite so noisy inside

and then he disappeared.

Narrative: Ali

a poem in twelve rounds

1.

My head so big
they had to pry
me out. I'm sorry
Bird (is what I call
my mother). Cassius
Marcellus Clay,
Muhammad Ali;
you can say
my name in any
language, any
continent: Ali.

2.

Two photographs
of Emmett Till,
born my year,
on my birthday.
One, he's smiling,
happy, and the other one
is after. His mother
did the bold thing,
kept the casket open,
made the thousands look upon
his bulging eyes,
his twisted neck,
her lynched black boy.
I couldn't sleep
for thinking,
Emmett Till.

One day I went
down to the train tracks,
found some iron
shoe-shine rests
and planted them
between the ties
and waited
for a train to come,
and watched the train
derail, and ran,
and after that
I slept at night.

3.

I need to train
around people,
hear them talk,
talk back. I need
to hear the traffic,
see people in
the barbershop,
people getting
shoe shines, talking,
hear them talk,
talk back.

4.

Bottom line: Olympic gold
can't buy a black man
a Louisville hamburger
in nineteen-sixty.

Wasn't even real gold.
I watched the river
drag the ribbon down,
red, white, and blue.

5.

Laying on the bed,
praying for a wife,
in walk Sonji Roi.

Pretty little shape.
Do you like
chop suey?

Can I wash your hair
underneath
that wig?

Lay on the bed,
Girl. Lie
with me.

Shake to the east,
to the north,
south, west—

but remember,
remember, I need
a Muslim wife. So

Quit using lipstick.
Quit your boogaloo.
Cover up your knees

like a Muslim
wife, religion,
religion, a Muslim

wife. Eleven
months with Sonji,
first woman I loved.

6.

There's not
too many days
that pass that I
don't think
of how it started,
but I know
no Great White Hope
can beat
a true black champ.
Jerry Quarry
could have been
a movie star,
a millionaire,
a senator,
a president—
he only had
to do one thing,
is whip me,
but he can't.

7. *Dressing-Room Visitor*

He opened
up his shirt:
"KKK" cut
in his chest.
He dropped
his trousers:
latticed scars
where testicles
should be. His face
bewildered, frozen,
in the Alabama woods
that night in 1966
when they left him
for dead, his testicles
in a Dixie cup.
You a warning,
they told him,
to smart-mouth,
sassy-acting niggers,
meaning niggers
still alive,
meaning any nigger,
meaning niggers
like me.

8. *Training*

Unsweetened grapefruit juice
will melt my stomach down.
Don't drive if you can walk,
don't walk if you can run.
I add a mile each day
and run in eight-pound boots.

My knuckles sometimes burst
the glove. I let dead skin
build up, and then I peel it,
let it scar, so I don't bleed
as much. My bones
absorb the shock.

I train in three-minute
spurts, like rounds: three
rounds big bag, three speed
bag, three jump rope, one-
minute breaks,
no more, no less.

Am I too old? Eat only
kosher meat. Eat cabbage,
carrots, beets, and watch
the weight come down:
two-thirty, two-twenty,
two-ten, two-oh-nine.

9.

Will I go
like Kid Paret,
a fractured
skull, a ten-day
sleep, dreaming
alligators, pork
chops, saxophones,
slow grinds, funk,
fishbowls, lightbulbs,
bats, typewriters,
tuning forks, funk,
clocks, red rubber
ball, what you see
in that lifetime
knockout minute
on the cusp?
You could be
let go,
you could be
snatched back.

10. *Rumble in the Jungle*

Ali boma ye,
Ali boma ye,
means kill him, Ali,
which is different
from a whupping
which is what I give,
but I lead them chanting
anyway, *Ali*
boma ye, because
here in Africa
black people fly
planes and run countries.

I'm still making up
for the foolishness
I said when I was
Clay from Louisville,
where I learned Africans
lived naked in straw
huts eating tiger meat,
grunting and grinning,
swinging from vines,
pounding their chests—

I pound my chest but of my own accord.

11.

I said to Joe Frazier,
first thing, get a good house
in case you get crippled
so you and your family
can sleep somewhere. Always
keep one good Cadillac.
And watch how you dress
with that cowboy hat,
pink suits, white shoes—
that's how pimps dress,
or kids, and you a champ,
or wish you were, 'cause
I can whip you in the ring
or whip you in the street.
Now back to clothes,
wear dark clothes, suits,
black suits, like you the best
at what you do, like you
President of the World.
Dress like that.
Put them yellow pants away.
We dinosaurs gotta
look good, gotta sound
good, gotta be good,
the greatest, that's what
I told Joe Frazier,
and he said to me,
We both bad niggers.
We don't do no crawlin'.

12.

They called me "the fistic pariah."

They said I didn't love my country,
called me a race-hater, called me out
of my name, waited for me
to come out on a stretcher, shot at me,
hexed me, cursed me, wished me
all manner of ill will,
told me that I was finished.

Here I am,
like the song says,
come and take me.

"The People's Champ,"

myself,
Muhammad.

Neonatology

Is
funky, is
leaky, is
a soggy, bloody crotch, is
sharp jets of breast milk shot straight across the room,
is gaudy, mustard-colored poop, is
postpartum tears that soak the baby's lovely head.

Then everything dries and disappears
Then everything dries and disappears
                              Neonatology
is day into night into day,
light into dark into light, semi-
and full-fledged, hyperconscious,
is funky, is funny: the baby farts,
we laugh. The baby burps, we smile, say "Yes."
The baby poops, his whole body stiffens,
then steam heat floods the pipes.
He slashes his nose with nails we cannot bear to trim,
takes a nap, and the wounds disappear.
The spirit lives in your squirts and coos.
Your noises and fluids are what you do.
                              Neonatology
is what we cannot see: you speak to the birds,
the birds speak back, is solemn,
singing, funky, frightening,
buckets of tears on the baby's lovely head, is

spongy.

"One day you'll forget the baby," Mother says,
"as if he were a pocketbook, a bag of groceries,
something you leave on a kitchen countertop.
I left you once, put on my coat and hat,
remembered my pocketbook, the top and bottom locks,
got all the way to the elevator before I realized.

It only happens once."

We lay on the bed and we rode the gray waves,
apricot juice in a glass in your hand,
single color in this gray light like November.
It is April. We rock.

Then the miracle which is always a miracle happens in many stages,

then the mouth which opens,
the bluebell
that sings.

I was just pregnant,
am no longer pregnant,
see myself in my memory
in overalls, sensible shoes.

Shockingly vital, mammoth giblet,
the second living thing to break free
of my body in fifteen minutes.

The midwife presents it on a platter.
We do not eat, have no Tupperware
to take it home and sanctify a tree.

Instead, we marvel at my cast-off meat,
the almost-pulsing slab, bloody mesa,
what lived moments ago, and now has died.

Now I must take the baby to my breast.
There is no mother here but me.
The midwife discards the placenta.

What do you make of this rain, little one,
night rain that your parents have loved all their lives?

From 2 to 3 *The Streets of San Francisco* comes on each night,
and I watch Karl Malden stop crime, and listen

to the mouse-squeak of your suckling, behold your avid jaws,
your black eyes: otter, ocelot,

my whelp, my cub, my seapup.
In the days before you smile at me

or call me Mama or love me,
love is all tit, all wheat-smelling milk, humid crook of the arm

where your warm damp head seems to live.
I pretend your clasping my finger means you love me.

Dreamt the baby
was born again,
arrived this time in a Moses basket,
had a crone's face,
a Senegalese head wrap,
a pendulous lower lip.

Mamma Zememesh, I dreamt your sister's names.
They floated around me as objects, satellites:

Zayd
      Ntutu
            Yeshareg
                  Asefash
                        Moulounesh

a spinning, turning, turning, spin.

I think the baby needs to eat. The baby's hungry.
Look! He's making sucking noises. Look!
His fist is in his mouth.
Why does the baby sleep all day? How
does the baby sleep at night? Three feedings? Hunh.
You need to let that baby cry.
You need to pick that baby up.
You need to put that baby down.
Kiss the baby too much, he'll get heartburn.
What are those bumps on the baby's face?
Why is the baby crying so?
That baby needs to eat, and now.

I dream the OB-GYN is here
to spend the night with us. He wears
his white coat and his stethoscope
to bed, looks like a loaf
of whole wheat bread. Good-night, we say,
and shut our eyes.
                              The next day
he's up early, jolly. "Time
to have this baby! Tally-ho!" And so we do.

All of my aunties chatting like crows on a line,
all of my aunties on electric breast pumps,
the double kind, one for each exhausted tit.

Mommy, the baby's head popped off! A tiny head,
white, wet, bloodless, heartbeat still on the soft spot.
She tells me, Stick it back on, Girl. Don't be afraid.

You can't show your children you're afraid.

A paraffin seam bubbles on his scalp.
A pink cicatrix lines his lovely neck.

Giving birth is like jazz, something from silence,
then all of it. Long, elegant boats,
blood-boiling sunshine, human cargo,
a handmade kite—

               Postpartum.
No longer a celebrity, pregnant lady, expectant.
It has happened; you are here,
each dram you drain a step away
from flushed and floating, lush and curled.
Now you are the pink one, the movie star.
It has happened. You are here,

and you sing, mewl, holler, peep,
swallow the light and bubble it back,
shine, contain multitudes, gleam. You

are the new one, the movie star,
and birth is like jazz,
from silence and blood, silence
then everything,

jazz.

From

American Sublime

(2005)

Emancipation

Corncob constellation,
oyster shell, drawstring pouch, dry bones.

Gris gris in the rafters.
Hoodoo in the sleeping nook.
Mojo in Linda Brent's crawlspace.

Nineteenth century corncob cosmogram
set on the dirt floor, beneath the slant roof,
left intact the afternoon
that someone came and told those slaves

"We're free."

Smile

When I see a black man smiling
like that, nodding and smiling
with both hands visible, mouthing

"Yes, Officer," across the street,
I think of my father, who taught us
the words "cooperate," "officer,"

to memorize badge numbers,
who has seen black men shot at
from behind in the warm months north.

And I think of the fine line—
hairline, eyelash, fingernail paring—
the whisper that separates

obsequious from *safe*. Armstrong,
Johnson, Robinson, Mays.
A woman with a yellow head

of cotton candy hair stumbles out
of a bar at after-lunchtime
clutching a black man's arm as if

for her life. And the brother
smiles, and his eyes are flint
as he watches all sides of the street.

Tina Green

Small story, hair story, Afro-American story,
only-black-girl-in-my-class story,
pre-adolescence story, black-teacher story.

"Take your hair out," they beg on the playground,
the cool girls, the straight-and-shiny-hair girls,
the girls who can run.

                    "Take your hair out," they say.
It is Washington hot, we are running, I do,
and it swells, snatches up at the nape, levitates,

woolly universe, knotting, fleece zeppelin, run.
So I do, into school, to the only black teacher
I'll have until college, the only black teacher

I've had to that point, the only black teacher
to teach at that school full of white people
who (tell the truth) I love, the teacher I love,

whose name I love, whose hair I love,
takes me in the teacher's bathroom and wordlessly
fixes my hair, perfectly, wordlessly

fixes my hair into three tight plaits.

When

In the early 1980s, the black men
were divine, spoke French, had read everything,
made filet mignon with green peppercorn sauce,
listened artfully to boyfriend troubles,
operatically declaimed boyfriend troubles,
had been to Bamako and Bahia,
knew how to clear bad humours from a house,
had been to Baldwin's villa in Saint-Paul,
drank espresso with Soyinka and Senghor,
kissed hello on both cheeks, quoted Baraka's
"Black Art": "Fuck poems/and they are useful,"
tore up the disco dance floor, were gold lit,
photographed well, did not smoke, said "Ciao,"

then all the men's faces were spotted.

Five Elegies

1. Poet's Tale

The older poet, he who would die soon after,
made me swig whiskey from his sacred silver flask
in the dark wings of the famous New York theater
before my maiden performance there, on jazz night,
to honor who else but happy birthday, Doctor King.
The great drummer drummed, great piano player played.
When the young one came out on the bass the older poet
leaned in so close that I could smell the spirits
and whispered, "Don't miss this one. This kid."

                                    He played
and he played, and he was not to be missed, the kid
who played the bass like conjuration. *Don't miss this one,*
and how did he know, the older poet, that I would not miss,
that he was pointing to a man I would love from that night forward.
What did he know when he made me swig for bravery,
pushed me out from behind the black velvet curtains
where I was hiding my face and said "Now"?

2. Lynda Hull

The poet Lynda Hull, who I did not know well,
has died so of course I am remembering
first meeting her in the women's room of an Italian
restaurant in Chicago, where she spoke to me
in the mirror and said, "Us redheads got to stick together,"
both of us dyed and flagrant, red lipstick,
her miniature body fierce and healing.

Poets are only famous to each other.
She wrote in my copy of *Star Ledger* "Hoping
to spend more time with you in this city of divas
and big shoulders," and now she's gone
out like the meteor she was,
a scarlet hole burning and hissing behind,
leaving this bitch of a world for the next.

3. Dream

The father was not my father, rather
a dark-skinned negro TV actor who plays
mid-level lieutenants, is never in charge.
I am me, as are the children, as is mother,
whose face tightens and pales as I diminish.
In my close-up in the hospital corridor
I ask, What is wrong with me? Say, Tell me
how to fight. I have looked in the mirror,
seen my ravages, the face that time and again
will not do what I ask it to, the caul.
The sympathetic negro taps my temple to say,
This kind, he means of cancer, exits weeping.
Time for the terrible aria, the one where I say,
I CAN NOT LEAVE THEM, my children,
and THE ONLY THING I EVER WAS AFRAID OF,
which is almost true.

                 The poet Agha Shahid Ali
met that disease and then like a rose
blown open faced his death and died
after asking, in the shape of a poem,
Why must we ever?

4. Ornette Coleman and Thelonious Monk at Dinner

When people smoked, and it hung over the table like magic
or like wisps of the talk and the music between them,

chicken bones, the best Chateaux, Coca-Cola in glass, Monk's eyes
cut left, Ornette laughing at something off-camera,

safari suit and Savile Row bespoke, haberdashery
circa '72 and the black globe is damn near free.

Deep sounds in the cusp and shift, in the sour and the off-notes
you bang and you blow, in the butter, the biscuits, the bird carcass,

jelly, just what you wanted and all you can eat.

5. Billy Strayhorn Writes "Lush Life"

Empty ice-cream carton
in a kitchen garbage can.
Up all night with your mother.
He beat her again. Up all night
eating ice cream, you made your mother laugh.

                        ly
Life   is lone

Duke's hands on your shoulders,
you play it again. Cancer
eats moth holes through
you and you and you.

                        ly
Life   is lone

Speeding upstate in the backseat,
on the Taconic, cocktail
in one hand, book in another
as autumn leaves blur by.
This life, New York, piano,
love, then lonely, this life, love.

Stray

On the beach, close to sunset, a dog runs
toward us fast, agitated, perhaps feral,
scrounging for anything he can eat.
We pull the children close and let him pass.

Is there such a thing as a stray child? Simon asks.
Like if a mother had a child from her body
but then decided she wanted to be a different child's mother,
what would happen to that first child?

The dog finds a satisfying scrap and calms.
The boys break free and leap from rock to rock.
I was a stray man before I met your mother,
you say, but they have run on and cannot hear you.

How fast they run on, past the dark pool
your voice makes, our arms which hold them back.
I was a stray man before I met you,
you say. This time you are speaking to me.

Fried Apples

I saw my mother's father
but a few times in my life:

a large man who glittered
and made his own weather,

lived near, rarely visited,
died when I was ten.

The first time I became
a woman I thought I did not

want to know what he taught me
about loving a glittering man.

I became a woman again
and remembered my grandfather

standing at the stove, cooking
a pan of fried apples for us

one Sunday morning in summer,
and I began to take his measure.

The Dream That I Told My Mother-in-Law

In the room almost filled with our bed,
the small bedroom, the king-sized bed high up
and on casters so sometimes we would roll,
in the room in the corner of the corner
apartment on top of a hill so the bed would roll,
we felt as if we might break off and drift,
float, and become our own continent.
When your mother first entered our apartment
she went straight to that room and libated our bed
with water from your homeland. Soon she saw
in my cheeks the fire and poppy stain,
and soon thereafter on that bed came the boy.
Then months, then the morning I cracked first one
then two then three eggs in a white bowl
and all had double yolks, and your mother
(now our mother) read the signs. Signs everywhere,
signs rampant, a season of signs and a vial
of white dirt brought across three continents
to the enormous white bed that rolled
and now held three, and soon held four,
four on the bed, two boys, one man, and me,
our mother reading all signs and blessing our bed,
blessing our bed filled with babies, blessing our bed
through her frailty, blessing us and our bed,
blessing us and our bed.

                          She began to dream
of childhood flowers, her long-gone parents.
I told her my dream in a waiting room:
a photographer photographed women,
said her portraits revealed their truest selves.
She snapped my picture, peeled back the paper,
and there was my son's face, my first son, my self.
Mamma loved that dream so I told it again.

And soon she crossed over to her parents,
sisters, one son (War took that son.
We destroy one another), and women came
by twos and tens wrapped in her same fine white
bearing huge pans of stew, round breads, homemade wines,
and men came in suits with their ravaged faces
and together they cried and cried and cried
and keened and cried and the sound
was a live hive swelling and growing,
all the water in the world, all the salt, all the wails,
and the sound grew too big for the building and finally
lifted what needed to be lifted from the casket and we quieted
and watched it waft up and away like feather, like ash.
Daughter, she said, when her journey began, *You are a mother now,*
and you have to take care of the world.

Black Poets Talk about the Dead

"Like Toni," he said,
"who came plain as day
to my dream last night
in a gangster beret,
tangerine-colored suit,
thigh-high go-go boots,
she tipped that brim and said,
How ya like me now?"

"After Etheridge passed
I went to see his woman
with my daughter, who was six
at the time, and had loved him.
We slept in the room where he'd slept
and in the night my child woke up
and said, *I was talking*
to Etheridge just now.
Can't you smell his cigarettes?"

"After she left us, we felt Mom close—
she had passed but not crossed—
and those were good weeks.
Her soup in the freezer,
perfume in her handkerchiefs,
half-empty cups of her tea, grown cold.
But bit by bit she left and then was gone.
They do that so we can mourn.
They do that so we believe it.
It is what it is: wretched work,
that we who the dead leave behind must do."

The African Picnic

World Cup finals, France v. Brasil.
We gather in Gideon's yard and grill.
The TV sits in the bright sunshine.
We want Brasil but Brasil won't win.
Aden waves a desultory green and yellow flag.
From the East to the West to the West to the East
we scatter and settle and scatter some more.
Through the window, Mamma watches from the cool indoors.

Jonah scarfs meat off of everybody's plate,
kicks a basketball long and hollers, "goal,"
then roars like the mighty lion he is.
Baby is a pasha surrounded by pillows
and a bevy of Horn of Africa girls
who coo like lovers, pronounce his wonders,
oil and massage him, brush his hair.
My African family is having a picnic, here in the USA.

Who is here and who is not?
When will the phone ring from far away?
Who in a few days will say good-bye?
Who will arrive with a package from home?
Who will send presents in other people's luggage
and envelopes of money in other people's pockets?
Other people's children have become our children
here at the African picnic.

In a parking lot, in a taxi-cab,
in a winter coat, in an airport queue,
at the INS, on the telephone,
on the cross-town bus, on a South Side street,
in a brand-new car, in a djellaba,
with a cardboard box, with a Samsonite,
with an airmail post, with a bag of spice,
at the African picnic people come and go.

The mailman sees us say good-bye and waves
with us, good-bye, good-bye, as we throw popcorn,
ululate, ten or twelve suitcases stuffed in the car.
Good-bye, Mamma, good-bye—
The front door shut. The driveway bare.
Good-bye, Mamma, good-bye.
The jet alights into the night,
a huge, metal machine in flight,
Good-bye, Mamma, good-bye.
At the African picnic, people come and go
and say good-bye.

Autumn Passage

On suffering, which is real.
On the mouth that never closes,
the air that dries the mouth.

On the miraculous dying body,
its greens and purples.
On the beauty of hair itself.

On the dazzling toddler:
"Like eggplant," he says,
when you say "Vegetable,"

"Chrysanthemum" to "Flower."
On his grandmother's suffering, larger
than vanished skyscrapers,

September zucchini,
other things too big. For her glory
that goes along with it,

glory of grown children's vigil,
communal fealty, glory
of the body that operates

even as it falls apart, the body
that can no longer even make fever
but nonetheless burns

florid and bright and magnificent
as it dims, as it shrinks,
as it turns to something else.

Ars Poetica #1,002: Rally

I dreamed a pronouncement
about poetry and peace.

"People are violent,"
I said through the megaphone

on the quintessentially
frigid Saturday

to the rabble stretching
all the way up First.

"People do violence
unto each other

and unto the earth
and unto its creatures.

Poetry," I shouted, "Poetry,"
I screamed, "Poetry

changes none of that
by what it says

or how it says, none.
But a poem is a living thing

made by living creatures
(live voice in a small box)

and as life
it is all that can stand

up to violence."
I put down the megaphone.

The first clap I heard
was my father's,

then another, then more,
wishing for the same thing

in different vestments.
I never thought, why me?

I had spoken a truth
offered up by ancestral dreams

and my father understood
my declaration

as I understood the mighty man
still caught in the vapor

between this world and that
when he said, "The true intellectual

speaks truth to power."
If I understand my father

as artist, I am free,
said my friend, of the acts

of her difficult father.
So often it comes down

to the father, his showbiz,
while the mother's hand

shapes us, beckons us
to ethics, slaps our faces

when we err, soothes
the sting, smoothes the earth

we trample daily, in light
and in dreams. Rally

all your strength, rally
what mother and father

together have made:
us on this planet,

erecting, destroying.

Ars Poetica #17: First Afro-American Esperantist

Gumbo ya-ya, lingua franca,
truffle or frango. Epic,
Affrilachia.

                    Oh language,
my trinket, my dialect bucket,
my bracelet of flesh.

Certificate: Esperantist.
Heirloom trunk, then Beinecke.
X-ray. Communicado. Acid-free.

Ars Poetica #28: African Leave-Taking Disorder

The talk is good. The two friends linger
at the door. Urban crickets sing with them.

There is no *after* the supper and talk.
The talk is good. These two friends linger

at the door, half in, half out, 'til one
decides to walk the other home. And so

they walk, more talk, the new doorstep, the
nightgowned wife who shakes her head and smiles

from the bedroom window as the men talk
in love and the crickets sing along.

The joke would be if the one now home
walked the other one home, where they started,

to keep talking, and so on: "African
Leave-Taking Disorder," which names her children

everywhere trying to come back together and talk.

Ars Poetica #23: "Whassup G?"

From the Latin *negrorum,* meaning
"to tote," said Richard Pryor
in an etymological mode.

Look it up in Cab Calloway's
Hepster's Dictionary, that giant book.
Be negro, be 'groid, be vernacular, be.

Hey, yo, Hey bro', Hey blood,
high five, big ups, gimme some skin,
keep it on the QT, the down low, the real side.

What it is? What it look like?
Vernacular: Verna, a house-born slave.
Ask your mama what it means.

Old school lyin' and signifyin'.
That chick has a chemical deficiency:
no assatol.

   And who knows,
on the radio, *what evil lurks*
in the hearts of men? The shadow do,

quoth the brethren, and fall out,
cack-a-lacking and slapping,
high-top fade to black.

Ars Poetica #21: Graduate Study of Literature

Shoebox full of chicken.
Darned sock, repaired picket fence.
A red front yard singing,
geranium pots lined up.

Pennies rolled and ready,
canvas tote bag of second-hand books.
Baltimore Avenue Trolley,
tofu from the corner Koreans.

Mending pile, hand-wash pile,
dry clean pile, Salvation Army pile.
Read so much you need new glasses.
Geraniums in the front yard singing:

"I am hand-made! I am home-grown!
You have not come outside in three days!"
Wash yourself in the following order:
face, pits, puss, behind.

Look inside my workman's lunch pail:
hard-boiled egg, salt in a tinfoil square,
carrot sticks, nectarine, chicken leg,
chocolate chip cookie or brownie.

Books, books, and talking about them.
Books, books, and talking about them,
and trolleying home to a third floor
walk-up and looking out the window

with bad eyes that can nonetheless
see the red of the geraniums,
the street pageantry that sings
and shuns, summons and sends away.

Ars Poetica #92: Marcus Garvey on Elocution

Elocution means to speak out.
That is to say, if you have a tale to tell,
tell it and tell it well.

This I was taught.

To speak properly you must have sound and good teeth.
You must have clear nostrils.
Your lungs must be sound.
Never try to make a speech on a hungry stomach.

Don't chew your words but talk them out plainly.
Always see that your clothing is properly arranged before you get on a platform.
You should not make any mistakes in pronouncing your words
because that invites amusement for certain people.

To realize I was trained for this,
expected to speak out, to speak well.
To realize, my family believed
I would have words for others.

An untidy leader is always a failure.
A leader's hair should always be well kept.
His teeth must also be in perfect order.
Your shoes and other garments must also be clean.
If you look ragged, people will not trust you.

My father's shoe-shine box:
black Kiwi, cordovan Kiwi,
the cloths, the lambswool brush.

My grandmother's dressing table:
potions for disciplining
anything scraggle or stray.

For goodness sake, always speak out,

said Marcus Garvey,
said my parents,
said my grandparents,
and meant it.

Ars Poetica #56: "Bullfrogs Was Falling Out of the Sky"

(Bundini Brown)

Not frogs but bullfrogs,
not rain but fat rain,
not Congo but Zaire
and Mobutu Sese Seko,

Mobutu Sese Seko,
his solid gold toilet seat,
leopard-skin fez,
international airstrip.

Not stealing but plundering,
Not Congo, Zaire. Not Drew
but Bundini, not Baptist
but Jew.

Not Cassius,
Muhammad, not Jesus,
Allah, the Koran,
the Bible, the Bible is black.

Do like it says on the mayonnaise jar:
keep cool but do not freeze.
Do like it says on the mayonnaise jar,
keep cool but do not freeze.

Not Afro but Afri-
ca, booty but plunder,
rain that astonishes,
rain like bullfrogs.

Mobutu, Mobutu,
both booty and plunder.
Oh Africa, Africa,
God in the rain.

Ars Poetica #16: Lot

During the Middle Passage
the captives drew lots for everything—

rations, labor, sleeping space—

I drew a laminated card
that read "Countee Cullen."

Here I am.

Ars Poetica #100: I Believe

Poetry, I tell my students,
is idiosyncratic. Poetry

is where we are ourselves
(though Sterling Brown said

"Every 'I' is a dramatic 'I'"),
digging in the clam flats

for the shell that snaps,
emptying the proverbial pocketbook.

Poetry is what you find
in the dirt in the corner,

overhear on the bus, God
in the details, the only way

to get from here to there.
Poetry (and now my voice is rising)

is not all love, love, love,
and I'm sorry the dog died.

Poetry (here I hear myself loudest)
is the human voice,

and are we not of interest to each other?

Ars Poetica #88: Sublime

In a pickle, we talk our way out
of our corners. We can the rough stuff.
Overture, theme and variation,
call and response, "I" equals "we."

Girl could *talk*. Sweet or savory?
Nutmeg or cinnamon? Jalapeno
or scotch bonnet? Maraschino
cherry or angostura bitters?

Sing, your mouth an O
which bubbles, tra la la,
or reaches low
to where *Nobody knows.*

What a baby knows:
the word as light,
the word as vowel,
the word as element,

the need to sing.

Amistad

Amistad

After the tunnel of no return
After the roiling Atlantic, the black Atlantic, black and mucilaginous
After the skin to skin in the hold and the picked handcuff locks
After the mutiny
After the fight to the death on the ship
After picked handcuff locks and the jump overboard
After the sight of no land and the zigzag course
After the Babel which settles like silt into silence
and silence and silence, and the whack
of lashes and waves on the side of the boat
After the half cup of rice, the half cup of sea-water
the dry swallow and silence
After the sight of no land
After two daughters sold to pay off a father's debt
After Cinque himself a settled debt

After, white gulf between stanzas

the space at the end

the last quatrain

The Blue Whale

swam alongside the vessel for hours.
I saw her breach. The spray when she sounded
soaked me (the lookout) on deck. I was joyous.
There her oily, rainbowed, lingering wake,
ambergris print on the water's sheer skin,
she skimmed and we skimmed and we sped
straight on toward home, on the glorious wind.

Then something told her, Turn (whales travel
in pods and will beach themselves rather than split)—
toward her pod?—and the way she turned was not
our way. I begged and prayed and begged for her
companionship, the guide-light of her print,
North Star (I did imagine) of her spout.
But she had elsewhere to go. I watched
the blue whale's silver spout. It disappeared.

Absence

In the absence of women on board,
when the ship reached the point where no landmass
was visible in any direction
and the funk had begun to accrue—
human funk, spirit funk, soul funk—who
commenced the moaning? Who first hummed that deep
sound from empty bowels, roiling stomachs,
from back of the frantically thumping heart?
In the absence of women, of mothers,
who found the note that would soon be called "blue,"
the first blue note from one bowel, one throat,
joined by dark others in gnarled harmony.
Before the head-rag, the cast-iron skillet,
new blue awaited on the other shore,
invisible, as yet unhummed. Who knew
what note to hit or how? In the middle
of the ocean, in the absence of women,
there is no deeper deep, no bluer blue.

boy haiku

the motherless child
rests his hand on a dead man's
forehead 'til it cools.

Poro Society

Without leopard skin, leather,
antelope horns, wart-hog tusks,
crocodile jaws, raffia muffs,

without the sacred bush,
the primordial grove,
our ancient initiations,

we must find a way
to teach the young man
on board with us.

We contend
with the forces of evil
in the universe.

Aggressive magic
addresses the need for control
in an imperfect world.

Approach

With shore in sight, the wind dies and we slow.
Up from the water bobs a sleek black head
with enormous dark eyes that question us:

who and what are you? Why? Then another
and another and another of those
faces, 'til our boat is all surrounded.

The dark creatures are seen to be
seals, New England gray seals, we later learn.
They stare. We stare. Not all are blackest black:

some piebald, some the dull gray of the guns
our captors used to steal and corral us,
some the brown-black of our brothers, mothers,

and two milky blue-eyed albino pups.
Albino: the congenital absence
of normal pigmentation. Something gone

amiss. Anomaly, aberration.

Connecticut

They squint from shore
at scarlet-shirted blackamoors.

The battered boat sails in.
White sky, black sea, black skin,

a low black schooner,
armed black men on deck

in shawls, pantaloons,
a Cuban planter's hat—

parched, starved,
dressed in what they found

in the dry goods barrels,
the Africans squint

at trees not their trees,
at shore not their shore.

Other Cargo

Saddles and bridles,
bolts of ribbon,
calico, muslin, silk,
beans, bread, books,
gloves, raisins, cologne,
olives, mirrors, vermicelli,
parasols, rice, black bombazine.

Education

In 1839, to enter University,
the Yale men already knew Cicero,

Dalzel's *Graeca Minora,* then learned more Latin prosody,
Stiles on astronomy, Dana's mineralogy.

Each year they named a Class Bully
who would butt heads with sailors in town.

"The first foreign heathen ever seen,"
Obookiah, arrived from Hawaii in '09.

The most powerful telescope in America
was a recent gift to the school

and through it, they were first to see
the blazing return of Halley's comet.

Ebeneezer Peter Mason
and Hamilton Lanphere Smith

spent all their free time at the instrument
observing the stars, their systems,

their movement and science and magic,
pondering the logic of mysteries that twinkle.

Some forty years before, Banneker's
eclipse-predicting charts and almanacs

had gone to Thomas Jefferson
to prove "that nature has given our brethren

talents equal to other colors of men."
Benjamin Banneker, born free,

whose people came from Guinea,
who taught himself at twenty-two (the same age

as the graduates) to carve entirely from wood
a watch which kept exquisite time,

accurate to the blade-sharp second.

The Yale Men

One by one the Yale men come
to teach their tongue to these
caged Africans so they might tell

in court what happened on the ship
and then, like Phillis Wheatley,
find the Yale men's God

and take Him for their own.

Teacher

(*Josiah Willard Gibbs*)

I learn to count in Mende one to ten,
then hasten to the New York docks to see
if one of these black seamen is their kind.

I run to one and then another, count.
Most look at me as though I am quite mad.
I've learned to count in Mende one to ten!

I shout, exhausted as the long day ends
and still no hope to know the captive's tale.
Is any of these black seamen their kind?

I'd asked an old Congo sailor to come
to the jail, but his tongue was the wrong one,
I learned. To count in Mende one to ten

begin *eta, fili, kian-wa, naeni.*
I spy a robust fellow loading crates.
Is this the black seaman who is their kind?

He stares at me as though I am in need,
but tilts his head and opens up his ear
and counts to me in Mende one to ten,
this one at last, this black seaman, their kind.

Translator

     (James Covey)

I was stolen from Mendeland as a child
then rescued by the British ship *Buzzard*
and brought to Freetown, Sierra Leone.

I love ships and the sea, joined this crew
of my own accord, set sail as a teen,
now re-supplying in New York Harbor.

When the white professor first came to me
babbling sounds, I thought he needed help
until *weta,* my mother's *six,* hooked my ear

and I knew what he was saying, and I knew
what he wanted in an instant, for we had heard
wild tales of black pirates off New London,

the captives, the low black schooner like
so many ships, an infinity of ships fatted
with Africans, men, women, children

as I was. Now it is my turn to rescue.
I have not spoken Mende in some years,
yet every night I dream it, or silence.

To New Haven, to the jail. To my people.
Who am I now? This them, not them. We burst
with joy to speak and settle to the tale:

We killed the cook, who said he would cook us.
They rubbed gunpowder and vinegar in our wounds.
We were taken away in broad daylight.

And in a loud voice loud as a thousand waves
I sing my father's song. It shakes the jail.
I sing from my entire black body.

Physiognomy

Monday, September 16, 1839
Another of the captured Africans named Bulwa (or Woolwah) died
on Saturday night. This is the third who has died in this city, and
the thirteenth since leaving Havana. One more remains sick in
this city the others having been removed to Hartford on Saturday, to
await their trial on Tuesday the 17th. Several are still affected with
the white flux, the disease which has proved fatal to so many of them.
                    The Daily Herald, New Haven

Kimbo, 5 feet 6 inches, with mustaches and long beard,
in middle life, calls himself Manding. Very intelligent,

he counts thus: 1. *eta,* 2. *fili,* 3. *kian-wa,* 4. *naeni,*
5. *loelu,* 6. *weta,* 7. *wafura,* 8. *wayapa,*
9. *ta-u,* 10. *pu.*

Shuma, 5 feet 6 inches, spoke
over the corpse of Tha
after Reverend Mister Bacon's prayer.

Konoma, 5 feet 4 inches, with incisor teeth
pressed outward and filed, with large lips
and projecting mouth, tattooed on the forehead,

calls himself Congo (Congo
of Ashmun's map of Liberia,
or Kanga, or Vater).

They are represented by travelers as handsome.
They are supposed to be more ancient of the soil than Timaris.
Their language, according to Port Chad, is distinct from any other.

Biah, 5 feet 4-1/2 inches with remarkably pleasant countenance,
with hands whitened by scars from gunpowder,
calls himself Duminah (Timari),

counts also in Timari.
He counts in Bullom thus.
He counts in Manding like Kwong.

With face broad in the middle
With sly and mirthful countenance (rather old)
With full Negro features
With hair shorn in rows from behind
With permanent flexion of two fingers on right hand
A mere boy, calls himself Manding
With depression of skull from a forehead wound
Tattooed on breast
With narrow and high head
With large head and high cheekbones
Marked on face by the smallpox
Stout and fleshy

Teme, 4 feet 3 inches, a young girl,
calls herself Congo but when further interrogated
says her parents were Congo, she a Manding.

Observe that in this examination
no one when asked for his name
gave any other than an African name.

No one when asked
to count counted in any
language other than African.

There was no appearance in any of them,
so far as I could judge,
of having been from Africa more than two or three months.

Constitutional

Mary Barber's children beg their mother
to take them into town each day to see
the Africans on the New Haven Green
let out of their cells for movement and air.

A New York shilling apiece to the jailer
who tucks away coins in a full suede purse.
The children push through skirts, past waistcoats,
to see the Africans turn somersets.

In the open air, in the bright sunlight,
the Africans chatter, and sound to
the children like blackbirds or cawing gulls.
The Africans spring. The Africans do not smile.

Mende Vocabulary

they
my father
our father
your father
my mother
our mother
my book
his house
one ship
two men
all men
good man
bad man
white man
black man

I eat
he eats
we eat
they sleep
I see God
did I say it right?
we sleep
I make
he makes
they have eaten

this book is mine
that book is his
this book is ours
I am your friend
here
now
that
there
then

The Girls

Margru, Teme, Kere,
the three little girls onboard.
In Connecticut
they stay with Pendleton
the jailer and his wife.
Some say they are slaves
in that house. The lawyer
comes to remove them,
but they cling to their hosts,
run screaming through the snow
instead of go. Cinque comes
and speaks in their language
with much agitation.
Do you fear Pendleton? *No.*
Do you fear the lawyer? *No.*
Do you fear Cinque? *No.*
Who or what do you fear?
The men, they say, *the men.*
The girls will become Christians.
They will move to Farmington
with the Mende mission
and return to Sierra Leone.
One will return to America
to attend college at Oberlin.
They will be called Sarah,
Maria, and Charlotte.

Kere's Song

My brother would gather the salt crust.
My grandmother would boil it gray to white.

My mother boated in the near salt river,
grabbed fat fish from the water with bare hands.

Women paint their faces with white clay and dance
to bring girls into our society, our

secrets, our womanhood, our community.
The clay-whitened faces of my mothers

are what I see in my dreams, and hear
drum-songs that drown girls' cries after

they have been cut to be made women.
If someone does evil, hags ride them

all night and pummel them to exhaustion.
Hags slip off their skins and leave them

in the corner during such rambles.
At my grandmother's grave, cooked chicken, red rice,

and water to sustain her on her journey.
I was learning the secrets of Sande

when they brought me here, before my dance,
before my drum, before my Sande song.

Judge Judson

These negroes are *bozals*
(those recently from Africa)
not *ladinos*

(those long on the island)
and were imported
in violation of the law.

The question remains:
What disposition shall be made
of these negroes?

Bloody may be their hands
yet they shall
embrace their kindred.

Cinqueze and Grabeau
shall not sigh for Africa
in vain

and once remanded
they shall no longer
be here.

In Cursive

Westville, February 9, 1841

Miss Chamberlain and others,

I will write you a few lines
because I love you very much
and I want you to pray to the great God to make us free
and give us new souls and pray for African people.

He sent his beloved son into the world
to save sinners who were lost. He sent
the Bible into the world to save us
from going down to Hell, to make us turn from sin.

I heard Mr. Booth say you give five dollars
to Mr. Townsend for African people. I thank you
and hope the great God will help you and bless you
and hear you and take you up to Heaven when you die.

I want you to pray to the great God make us free.
We want to go home and see our friends in African Country.
I want the great God love me very much and forgive all my sins.
All Mendi people thank you for your kindness.

Hope to meet you in Heaven. Your friend, Kale

God

There is one God in Farmington, Connecticut,
another in Mendeland.

None listen.
None laugh, but none have listened.

We will sail home carrying Bibles
and wearing calico.

The journey this time
is seven weeks.

If we find our mothers,
children, fathers, brothers,

sisters, aunties, uncles,
cousins, friends,

if we find them,
we will read to them

(we read this book)
the God stories in our Bibles.

That is the price for the ticket home
to Mendeland

for us the decimated three years hence.

Waiting for Cinque to Speak

Having tried,

having tried, having failed,

having raised rice
that shimmered green, green,
having planted and threshed.

Having been a man, having sired children,
having raised my rice, having amassed a bit of debt,
having done nothing remarkable.

Years later it would be said
the Africans were snatched into slavery, then,
that we were sold by our own into slavery, then,
that those of our own who sold us
never imagined chattel slavery,
the other side of the Atlantic.

Having amassed debt, I was taken to settle that debt.
(Not enough rice in the shimmering green.)
Better me than my daughter or son. (I was strong.)
And on the ship I met my day
as a man must meet his day.
Out of the Babel of Wolof and Kissee
we were made of the same flour and water, it happened.
On the ship, I met my day.

The Amistad *Trail*

The *Amistad* Trail bus
leaves from the commuter parking lot,
Exit 37 off Highway 84.
There is interest in this tale.

See where the girls lived while waiting
for the boat to sail home, see Cinque's room,
the Farmington church where they learned
to pray to Jesus, Foone's grave.

Good things: eventual justice, John Quincy Adams,
black fighting back, white helping black
Bad things: the fact of it, price of the ticket,
the footnote, the twist, and the rest—

Done took my blues
Done took my blues and

—the good and the bad of it.
Preach it: learn. Teach it: weep.

Done took my blues.
Done took my blues and gone.
The verse will not resolve.
The blues that do not end.

Cinque Redux

I will be called bad motherfucker.
I will be venerated.
I will be misremembered.
I will be Seng-Pieh, Cinqueze, Joseph,
and end up CINQUE.

I will be remembered
as upstart, rebel, rabble-rouser, leader.
My name will be taken by black men
who wish to be thought RIGHTEOUS.
My portrait will be called "The Black Prince."
Violent acts will be committed in my name.
My face will appear on Sierra Leonean currency.

I will not proudly sail the ship home
but will go home, where I will not sell slaves,
then will choose to sail off
to a new place: Jamaica, West Indies.
In America, they called us *"Amistads."*
The cook we killed, Celestino, was mulatto.
Many things are true at once.

Yes I drew my hand across my throat
in the courtroom, at that cur Ruiz
to hex his thieving, killing self.
Yes I scuffled here and there instead of immolate.
Yes I flaunted my gleam and spring.
No I did not smile.
No I never forgot the secret teachings
of my fathers. No I never forgot

who died on board, who died on land,
who did what to whom, who will die
in the future, which I see
unfurling like the strangest dream.

The Last Quatrain

and where now

and what now

the black white space

American Sublime

(At the same time, American paintings wherein
the biodynamic landscape explodes in flames,

ice, violent sunshine that seems to burn the canvas,
apocalyptic nature that roils and terrifies.

The Beautiful: small scale, gentle luminosity.
Sublime: territorial, vast, craggy, un-

domesticated, borderless, immense, unknown,
awful, monumental, transcendent, transcending.

Go West and West young man, to blinding snowstorms. Leave
shark-infested waters, shipwrecks without slaves.

Miraculous black holes of color large enough
to blot out the sun, obliterate the unending moans,

to exalt, to take the place of lamentation.)

Tanner's *Annunciation*

Gabriel disembodied,
pure column of light.

Humble Mary, receiving the word
that the baby she carries is God's.

Not good news, not news, even,
but rather the rightly enormous word,

Annunciation. She knew
they were chosen. She knew

he would suffer, as the chosen child
always suffers. Perhaps she knew

the dearest wish, mercy,
would be ever-inchoate,

like Gabriel: light that carries
possibility, illuminates,

but that can promise nothing but itself.

From

Miss Crandall's School for Young Ladies and Little Misses of Color

(2007)

Knowledge

It wasn't as if we knew nothing before.
After all, colored girls must know many
things in order to survive. Not only
could I sew buttons and hems, but I could
make a dress and pantaloons from scratch.
I could milk cows, churn butter, feed chickens,
clean their coops, wring their necks, pluck and cook them.
I cut wood, set fires, and boiled water
to wash the clothes and sheets, then wrung them dry.
And I could read the Bible. Evenings
before the fire, my family tired
from unending work and New England cold,
they'd close their eyes. My favorite was Song of Songs.
They most liked when I read, "In the beginning."

Good-bye

The mother who packs her daughter's valise,
tucks a Bible between the muslin layers.
The father who shoes horses and fixes
clocks and other intricate things that break
saves coins in their largest preserving jar
'til the day for which they have waited comes.
See Mother wash and oil and comb and braid
Daughter's thick brown hair for the very last time.

Does "good-bye" mean we hope or mean we weep?
Does it mean remember all you know, or
come back as soon as you can, or do not?
Does it mean go now, or I do not know?
Good-bye, Daughter, says Mother. She watches
the horse and buggy 'til it fades from view.

Study

Each day we study English grammar, spell
abdicate, alabaster, amplitude,
learn astronomy, geography, math,
French, and drawing in off-hours. Prayers.

After Mariah has finished her chores,
she takes off her apron and works with us
in time for our favorite book of all,
Peter Parley's Universal History.

"Suppose you could fly in a hot-air balloon,"
so in our minds we fly from our classroom
over land and water to Noah's ark,
"the Barbary States," Queen Semiramis,

to palaces, fortresses, sepulchers,
and the evil, the evil, that men do.

We

Colored are new to these townsfolk, who say
we have come to take white husbands, but we
are young girls who do not think of such things.
They see us horned, tailed, befeathered, with
enormous bottoms and jaws that snap, red-
devil eyes that could hex a man and make him
leave home. Though the state has said no to slavery,
we know how it happens with colored girls
and white men, their red-devil eyes and tentacles.
Our mothers have taught us remarkably
to blot out these fears, black them out, and flood
our minds with light and God's great face.
We think about that which we cannot see:
something opening wide and bright, a key.

Lawyers

If not citizens and protected as such,
they are aliens and shall be driven out
from our borders as Turks or Chinese.

If the power claimed exists, then the law
has the power to send each white youth at Yale
College out of our borders as aliens.

This American nation, this nation
of white men may be taken from us
and given to the African race!

Can we call back oceans of tears and
groans of millions of the Middle Passage?
I tell this honorable court that we
owe a debt to the colored population
that we can never repay, no, never.

Allegiance

Teacher is bewildered when packages
and letters come from far to say how brave,
how visionary, how stare-down-the-beast
is Prudence Crandall of Canterbury.
Work, she says, there is always work to do,
not in the name of self but in the name,
the water-clarity of what is right.
We crave radiance in this austere world,
light in the spiritual darkness.
Learning is the one perfect religion,
its path correct, narrow, certain, straight.
At its end it blossoms and billows
into vari-colored polyphony:

the sweet infinity of true knowledge.

Water

After the shunning came the vile words, then
cow dung in the water well, fouling it,
so none for us to wash with, clean with, drink.
Past every dusk we gather pails of snow.
Mariah boils it, cools it down in jugs,
and so we drink until the water clears.
To show our faces risks their clubs and stones.
We take our constitutionals inside,
twenty girls two abreast in line marching
up and down the stairs, 'round the well and back,
all windows wide open for cold, fresh air.
We thank God for the house we hide inside.
Bless the snow. Bless Mariah, Teacher Pru,
who talks to God and figures what to do.

Hunger

The flour tin has been empty for a month.
No one in town will sell us anything,
no milk, no flour, no salt, no eggs, no tea.

The townsfolk have invented their "Black Laws"
to drive us out, keep everyone away
so we will stop our learning, leave, or starve.
They celebrate their laws with cannon fire.

We girls are not accustomed to rough bread
but learn to eat loaves made from stone-ground meal
and drink tea from the many different weeds
Mariah and Sarah discuss and sort.

In the cellar summer kitchen, salt pork,
sacks of kidney beans, potatoes sprouting
eyes we'll bury in dirt inside, and tend.

Call and Response

Students:
Having heard the bellow of fire roaring
against this house, we hear it evermore
in our imaginations and night dreams.
So terror operates: there when it is
and there when it is not, ambient, dull
and insistent, indelible. We read,
work, walk, sing; we pray to vanquish the flames.

Prudence Crandall:
I have never met souls hungrier for
learning, that which splits the world akimbo,
is hope itself in the absence of grace.
Who would I be if I did not teach these
young ladies, little misses of color?
Know I will never no never turn back.
My girls, we must sail above the treetops.

Cat

Eliza finds the black-and-white striped cat
tethered to the front gate with its throat slit.
At first she considers telling no one,
finding Frederick's shovel and burying
the poor dead wretch in a backyard corner.
As her classmates, she has learned to handle
what comes as worse and worse comes, like Teacher
and every person she has ever known:
to keep her hand to the plow, eyes to God.
Today, though, this day, this stiff, splayed creature,
open-eyed, spilling viscera, is more
than Eliza can handle by herself.
She runs inside, screams the news. Eliza
is twelve years old. The cat is black and white.

End

Upturned stacks of Webster's blue-backed spellers.
Broken slates. *Liberators* burned to ash.
Ninety panes of first-floor windows smashed,
frame wood splintered and jagged as tinder.

I can no longer protect my students.
Strangely, it is not God's words that ring
in my head as I search for understanding,
rather, words that I saw on a charred reader:

I must remind you that the earth is round.
Men and animals live on the surface.
There is no comfort in these words,
yet the fact of them comforts me: schoolbooks.

I am a teacher of colored misses,
but can no longer protect my students.

Julia Williams

Looking back, I remember reading
legal papers into the night (though we
were conserving candles) and finding
no intricacies to unravel in their
familiar and inelegant arguments,
Canterbury v. Prudence Crandall.
They won that time, but we were not deterred.
I went on to Canaan, New Hampshire,
this time as a teacher to other eager
young of both races. From the town and neighbors
came three hundred armed men, ninety oxen teams.
They dragged the school building utterly off
its foundation. I have twice seen bloodlust
and ignorance combust. I have seen it.

New Poems

Luck

I ask Mommy what happened
to the coffee can of bacon grease
she kept by the side of the stove,
grease in which she cooked eggs,
sautéed pork chops, grease she saved
for sublime fried chicken, slicked on burns,
threw by the dollop in the greens pot.
We didn't eat like that every day,
but we ate like that, yes, we ate like that,
ate Black, despite, despite.
                                        Red beans
and rice, pot fulla knuckles, collards
on New Year's Day. Black-eyed peas
poured into a pot, the tinkling rush,
dinner to come, all-seeing eyes,
luck's music, this never-ending,
the emerald-green year spread before us
like nothing but its unseen self.

In D.C.

In D.C. there are black women
with golden Afros and African-
print jumpsuits. Sidewalks sizzle

in summer, a languid,
loving fizz, a *Hey Girl*
hissing from the streets,

ambient, *hey girl* on all sides. Walk
up and down Georgia Avenue
or Florida Avenue or Columbia Road:

How you doin'? Hey.
You never know what you will miss
when you leave, what will call you

back, what will disappear
forever, or what was never there
quite as you now see it, hear it, write it

in memory's poem.

The Black Woman Speaks

(Elizabeth Catlett)

I am thirty-two and the love of my life,
and my great work, and my three sons,

and my new nation are ahead of me. Good-bye, Chicago.
About to set out for the territory, Mexico,

for the rest of the century and into the next.
My sense of my people will strengthen and shift.

But first I had to leave D.C. You have to leave D.C.,
lovely colored town that will make a colored girl smile

but not stretch or growl or frown
with the exertion of thinking, WORK.

Yet there I made my first carving
from a cake of Ivory soap, at Dunbar High School.

There I was taught. There I stood
in front of the United States Supreme Court

with a noose around my neck, protesting lynching.
There I realized I had a debt I had not paid.

I am black because my great-great grandmother
was kidnapped on a beach in Madagascar.

In Mexico, I will carve black women's bodies and heads
from red stone and black stone. The work will make me sweat.

The black woman's head is a massive weight.
The black woman's head holds the black woman's brain.

The black woman's work is the work of this world.

Dream Book

(found poem, *Pettengill's Perfect Fortune-Teller
and Dream Book*, 1944)

NEGRO To dream of being frightened or assaulted by a negro is a good sign, as it denotes safety: if the negro comes toward you in a pleasant and agreeable way, it shows that you will meet with loss or be robbed: to see a grinning, pleasant-looking negro in your dream forebodes trouble through the conduct of a dependent.

POET If any young person should be so silly as to dream of writing poetry, it foretells poverty; and for one to dream of having a poetical lover or sweet-heart is a sign that they will fall in love with a fool: if a girl dreams that her lover writes verses to her beauty, she had better send him off at once unless she desires to marry a putty-head, for dreaming of such nonsense foretells a worse match than the reality.

Toomer

(Jean Toomer)

I did not wish to "rise above"
or "move beyond" my race. I wished

to contemplate who I was beyond
my body, this container of flesh.

I made up a language in which to exist.
I wondered what God breathed into me.

I wondered who I was beyond
this complicated, milk-skinned, genital-ed body.

I exercised it, watched it change and grow.
I spun like a dervish to see what would happen. Oh,

to be a Negro is—is?—
to be a Negro, is. To be.

In the Aquarium

Like a kiss from a perfect lover,
the jellyfish pulse and pulse,
like wishes, like migraine,
like perfect, fleeting thoughts.

No treachery in the aquarium.
Nothing can sting through glass.
Harmless, incipient
as a twelve-year-old's mustache.

Or maybe the pulse is not yearning,
the over and over of coming,
but how it keeps moving through water,
how jellyfish stay alive.

Bottle Tree

Not the cherry orchard but
the gold East African wheat field
for which you pine,

not rose but gold light,
your land, your land.
Not a gazebo

but the bottle tree
I want to end this poem,
glinting in the sun,

tinkling in the front-yard wind.

Hayden in the Archive

Stoop-shouldered, worrying the pages,
index finger moving down the log,
column by column of faded ink.

Blood from a turnip, this
protagonist-less
Middle Passage.

Does the log yield lyric?
The slavers' meticulous records,
elaborate hand,

the ship's names, that poetry,
crystalline ironies:
Amistad.

At times the dusty pages make him sneeze,
small sneezes, which he suppresses,
chew – chew – chew.

Repetition rampant,
Jesus – Jesus – Jesus,
the *row-row* and *heave-ho* on shipboard.

Hayden's satchel
is filled with bundles
of freshman compositions.

(The water, the girl,
eight children, newspaper,
the notes on a napkin.)

This morning, the poem insists.

Poised

Having become my grandmother
by always carrying a folding umbrella in my pocketbook,
by virtue of having reached the age
she was when I first knew her,

I always carry peanuts. Kleenex, spare pencils.
I now understand "just in case." I am the woman who
drills a finger in a child's mid-spine for posture. I wear
red lipstick, no longer buy cheap shoes.

I see who I have become when my child
parrots "Gracious!" or "Lord have mercy!"
I perch like a bird smack-dab in the middle
of a power-line: my life, half-coming, half-done.

Stokely and Adam

Stokely says, Now.
Adam says, Soon.

Stokely says, Straight ahead.
Adam says, To the side.

Stokely says, Black Power.
Adam says, Power.

Stokely says, Global.
Adam says, Harlem is the center of the world.

Stokely: Sweet potatoes.
Adam: Sweet potato pie.

Adam: Don't buy where you can't work.
Stokely: Freedom ride.

Stokely says, Yeah.
Adam says, Yeah.

Adam says, Preach. Stokely says, Talk.
Agitate, agitate, agitate.

Adam says, Inside the system.
Stokely says, The system will bite you in the ass.

Adam says, You think I don't know that?
Adam says, Even inside is outside.

Adam and Stokely:
Us black folks got to stick together.

Stokely: We had only the old language of love and suffering.
Adam: Keep the faith, baby.

Sugar in their eyes, ketchup in their hair, I was burning,
said Stokely Carmichael, witnessing the kids at the lunch counters.

Why I do what I do. Why I burn.
Why I work, said Adam Clayton Powell. Why I serve.

In the FEMA Trailers

One key worked on all of the doors
of all the FEMA trailers. One day

I came home from work and found banana peels
in my garbage from bananas I did not eat.

Sometimes we'd open the trailer door
and see we were surrounded by dogs:

wild dogs, pregnant dogs
with bellies hanging low,

looking for a bone, any scrap.
We'd close the door and wait inside

as long as it took for the dogs to go
which was sometimes hours.

We were two women in the FEMA trailer.
After some months, because we worked for the city,

they moved us to the docked cruise ship.
That's when she started drinking

and carrying on on deck
every night when we got home from work

(we were lucky to have work).
Some got like that from the stress

and from finally being with other people.
That's when I let my depression begin,

when the genie jumped out of the bottle.
I stayed in our cabin below deck,

listening to the louder and louder voices
above deck, listening to the laughing

get wilder, and wilder, and wilder.

Rally

(Miami, October 2008)

The awesome weight of the world had not yet descended
upon his athlete's shoulders. I saw someone light but not feathered

jog up to the rickety stage like a jock off the court
played my game   did my best

and the silent crowd listened and dreamed.
The children sat high on their parents' shoulders.

Then the crowd made noise that gathered and grew
until it was loud and was loud as the sea.

What it meant or would mean was not yet fixed
nor could be, though human beings ever tilt toward *we.*

Praise Song for the Day

Each day we go about our business,
walking past each other, catching each other's
eyes or not, about to speak or speaking.

All about us is noise. All about us is
noise and bramble, thorn and din, each
one of our ancestors on our tongues.

Someone is stitching up a hem, darning
a hole in a uniform, patching a tire,
repairing the things in need of repair.

Someone is trying to make music somewhere,
with a pair of wooden spoons on an oil drum,
with cello, boom box, harmonica, voice.

A woman and her son wait for the bus.
A farmer considers the changing sky.
A teacher says, *Take out your pencils. Begin.*

We encounter each other in words, words
spiny or smooth, whispered or declaimed,
words to consider, reconsider.

We cross dirt roads and highways that mark
the will of some one and then others, who said,
I need to see what's on the other side.

I know there's something better down the road.
We need to find a place where we are safe.
We walk into that which we cannot yet see.

Say it plain: that many have died for this day.
Sing the names of the dead who brought us here,
who laid the train tracks, raised the bridges,

picked the cotton and the lettuce, built
brick by brick the glittering edifices
they would then keep clean and work inside of.

Praise song for struggle, praise song for the day.
Praise song for every hand-lettered sign,
the figuring-it-out at kitchen tables.

Some live by *love thy neighbor as thyself*,
others by *first do no harm* or *take no more
than you need*. What if the mightiest word is love?

Love beyond marital, filial, national,
love that casts a widening pool of light,
love with no need to pre-empt grievance.

In today's sharp sparkle, this winter air,
any thing can be made, any sentence begun.
On the brink, on the brim, on the cusp,

praise song for walking forward in that light.

The Elders

watched him glitter,
watched him gleam,
shook his un-rough hands
with their cotton-scarred hands,
cut their eyes at him,
observed the ease with which he smiled,

asked, finally, what is love,
and who are The People
and how must we love them and what do we need,
what is now, look at the lines
in the corner of youngblood's eyes,
lined not unlike our hands,
and perhaps this is not gleam but illumination,
not merely his but ours.

One week later in the strange

One week later in the strange
exhilaration after Lucille's death

our eyes were bright as we received instructions,
lined up with all we were supposed to do.

Now seers, now grace notes, now anchors, now tellers,
now keepers and spreaders, now wide open arms,

the cold wind of generational shift
blew all around us, stinging our cheeks,

awakening us to the open space
now everywhere surrounding.

Notes

Amistad:

On July 2, 1839, a rebellion occurred aboard the Spanish slave schooner *Amistad* near the coast of Cuba. The *Amistad* was sailing from Havana to Puerto Principe, Cuba, when the ship's passengers, three girls, one boy, and thirty-nine men recently abducted from Sierra Leone, revolted. The captives, led by Joseph Cinque, killed the ship's captain and cook, but spared the navigator so that he would bring the ship back to Sierra Leone. Instead, the navigator sailed northward, where the United States Navy seized the *Amistad* off Long Island and towed it to New London, Connecticut. The captives were held in a jail in New Haven, Connecticut. There was great interest in their presence, including from Yale Professor Josiah Willard Gibbs, who brought his students to try to teach the captives English so that they might tell their story in court.

The Spanish demanded the return of the *Amistad* captives to Cuba. In 1840, a trial took place in a federal court in Hartford, Connecticut. New England abolitionist Lewis Tappan and others tried to organize sympathy for the captives, but the United States government sided with proslavery opinions. President Martin Van Buren ordered a Navy ship sent to Connecticut to return the Africans to Cuba. Nonetheless, the judge ruled that the captives were not merchandise, but were instead victims of kidnapping and had the right to escape their captors; he said they should be made free. The United States appealed the case before the Supreme Court the next year; congressman and former president John Quincy Adams argued in favor of the Africans. The Supreme Court upheld the lower court. Private and missionary society donations helped the thirty-five surviving Africans secure passage back to Sierra Leone, where they arrived in January 1842. Five missionaries and teachers hoping to found a Christian mission joined the Africans on this return.

Spain insisted that the United States pay indemnification for the ship. The United States Congress continued to debate the case until the beginning of the Civil War in 1861.

Miss Crandall's School for Young Ladies and Little Misses of Color:

In 1831, the citizens of Canterbury, Connecticut, approached twenty-eight-year-old Prudence Crandall and asked her to start a boarding school for young women, for which the town would purchase the grandest house in Canterbury. In its first year, the Canterbury Female Boarding School taught young white women in the area. After a young African American housekeeper named Mariah Davis began to attend classes, the townspeople objected. Parents of the white students were outraged at the thought of their daughters being taught alongside a black woman. If Mariah was allowed to continue attending classes, parents warned, they would withdraw their daughters from the school. Prudence Crandall would not balk, and as the white students left, the Canterbury Female Boarding School began to teach young black women exclusively. Crandall placed a notice in the abolitionist newspaper *The Liberator* advertising her school for "young ladies and little misses of color," and within a year, African American girls from Philadelphia to Providence began to arrive.

The town passed laws designed to force students to return to their homes and shut down the school. Miss Crandall was twice arrested, jailed, and tried in court as she continued to teach young black women. Crandall and her students faced daily humiliation. Stores refused to sell the young women provisions, and the town doctor refused them medical attention. Townspeople threw eggs and rocks at the school. Neighbors used animal dung to poison the school's water. Other violence ensued.

On September 9, 1834, townspeople surrounded the school, smashed the windows, ransacked the ground floor, and set the schoolhouse on fire. It was then that Crandall realized she could no longer protect her students, so she decided that her only choice was to close the school. She eventually left Connecticut and traveled west, settling in Kansas.

The Canterbury Female Boarding School was purchased in 1969 and is today a National Historic Landmark and museum.

Acknowledgments

"Toomer," "Hayden in the Archive," "Stokely and Adam," and "Rally" appeared in the *American Scholar*.

"Poised" first appeared in *PMS poemmemoirstory* number 8, edited by Honorée Fanonne Jeffers, in 2008.

"The Black Woman Speaks," "Toomer," and "Stokely and Adam" were first published in *Let Your Motto Be Resistance: African American Portraits*, edited by Deborah Willis and published by Smithsonian Books in 2007. These poems also appeared in the chapbook *Poems in Conversation and a Conversation* (with Lyrae Van Clief-Stafanon), published by Slapering Hol Press in 2008.

The author would like to thank the John Simon Guggenheim Foundation, the Alphonse Fletcher, Sr. Fellowship Program, the Jackson Poetry Prize (administered by Poets and Writers and established and supported by John and Susan Jackson), the Radcliffe Institute for Advanced Study (especially Judith Vichniac), the W.E.B. Du Bois Institute at Harvard University, and Yale University, all of whom have generously supported this work. Thanks also to the sparkling young women who have provided invaluable assistance over the years: Abe Louise Young, Sarah Weiss, Liba Wenig Rubenstein, Charita Gainey, Elisabeth Houston, and Erika Maki.

ELIZABETH ALEXANDER was born in New York City and raised in Washington, D.C. She is the author of five previous collections of poetry, *The Venus Hottentot, Body of Life, Antebellum Dream Book, American Sublime,* and *Miss Crandall's School for Young Ladies and Little Misses of Color* (co-authored with Marilyn Nelson). She is also the author of two collections of essays, *The Black Interior* and *Power and Possibility: Essays, Interviews, Reviews,* and she edited *The Essential Gwendolyn Brooks* and *Love's Instruments* by Melvin Dixon. Her poetry, short stories, and critical prose have been published in numerous periodicals and anthologies.

Alexander has read her work across the United States and in Europe, the Caribbean, and South America. On January 20, 2009, she delivered her poem "Praise Song for the Day" at the inauguration of President Barack Obama. She has appeared on CNN, the *Colbert Report,* and the PBS documentary series *Faces of America,* among other media and programs. She has received many awards and honors, including the Anisfield-Wolf Lifetime Achievement Award in Poetry, the Alphonse Fletcher, Sr. Fellowship for work that "contributes to improving race relations in American society and furthers the broad social goals of the U.S. Supreme Court's *Brown v. Board of Education* decision of 1954," and the 2007 Jackson Prize for Poetry from Poets and Writers. Her book *American Sublime* was one of two finalists for the 2005 Pulitzer Prize in Poetry.

Alexander is the chair of the Department of African American Studies at Yale University, and also teaches in the Cave Canem Poetry Workshop. She lives with her family in New Haven, Connecticut.

Crave Radiance has been set in Arno Pro, a typeface created by Robert Slimbach whose name refers to the river that runs through Florence and is based on early humanistic types of the Italian Renaissance. Book design by Rachel Holscher. Composition by BookMobile Design and Publishing Services, Minneapolis, Minnesota. Manufactured by Maple Vail on acid-free paper.